The Soccer Handbook
for Players, Coaches and Parents

The Soccer Handbook for Players, Coaches and Parents

ALBERT M. LUONGO

McFarland & Company, Inc., Publishers
Jefferson, North Carolina, and London

A special thanks to the Fédération
Internationale de Football Associations Board
for granting permission to reprint
the 1995 *Laws of the Game*

Sketches in this book are by Ann Marie Clarkson.
Diagrams are by Herbert Rego, Jr.

British Library Cataloguing-in-Publication data are available

Library of Congress Cataloguing-in-Publication Data

Luongo, Albert M., 1939–
The soccer handbook for players, coaches and parents /
Albert M. Luongo.
p.   cm.
Includes index.

ISBN-13: 978-0-7864-0159-8
(softcover : 50# alk. paper) ∞

1. Soccer — Handbooks, manuals, etc.
2. Soccer — Training — Handbooks, manuals, etc.
3. Soccer — Rules — Handbooks, manuals, etc.
I. Title.
GV943.L83   1996
796.334 — dc20   96-27651
CIP

Manufactured in the United States of America

*McFarland & Company, Inc., Publishers
Box 611, Jefferson, North Carolina 28640*

Table of Contents

List of Drawings, Photographs and Form   xi
Introduction   1

1. Getting Started   5
What Is Soccer About?   6
Leadership   9
Coach Development   11
Poor Quality Play   12
Important Areas of Control   13
Substitute Players   16
Can Parents Increase Their Child's Playing Time?   17
Aggression and Roughness   20
Conditioning and Injuries   21
Equipment   22
Clothing   23

2. Skill Level   25
Advice for the Beginning Coach   26
Suggested Guidelines for Practices   27
Better Play and Team Work   30
League Control   32
Parents' Participation   34
Expected or Average Skill Levels by Age   35
Under 10   36
Under 12   37
Under 14   39
Under 16   40
Under 19   41
Habits of Players with Style Not Skill   42

v

3. Basic Skills for Field Players — 45
Dribbling — 45
Basic Trapping — 48
Heading — 49
Shielding — 50
Receiving the Ball — 51
Dribbling — 51
Turning — 54
On the Touch Line — 56
A Final Note on Shielding — 56
Defending — 58
Body Traps — 61
Instep Kicks — 62
Push Passes — 64
The Chest Traps — 65
Throw-Ins — 66

4. Elements of the Game — 71
Players — 71
Goalkeeper — 72
Center Defense Person — 72
Sweeper Back — 72
Defensive Wingers — 73
Center Halfbacks — 73
Wing Halfbacks — 74
Right and Left Forward Wingers — 75
Center Forwards — 76
Soccer Formations — 76
W-M Formation — 78
4-3-3 Formation — 79
3-3-4 Formation — 80
4-4-2 Formation — 81
3-2-5 Formation — 81
General Attacking and Defending — 82
Defensive Strategy — 86
The Goalkeeper's Role — 87
Attack Soccer vs. Defensive Soccer — 89
Ball Control — 90

Plays   91
   Kickoff   91
   Wall Pass   92
   Defensive Play on Throw-Ins   93
   Cross for Shots on Goal   93
   Corner Kicks   94
   Goal Kicks   95
   Shot on Goal Follow-up   96
   Fakes   96
   Trapping in Front of the Goal   97
   Breakaways   98
   Setting Up Walls   99
   Drawing Off Players   100
   Scoring   100
   Penalty Kicks   101
      Offensive Play   101
      Defensive Play   102
Referees   103
   The Three- and Two-Person Systems   105
   Preparation for Games   107
   The Offside Law   108
   Coaches' Evaluation of Referees   108

5. Goalkeeping   111
   Goalie's Stance   114
   Catching in the Air   114
   Positioning   115
   Punching   118
   Tipping   119
   Catching Low and Direct Balls   120
   Lunging   121
   Punting   122
   Goal Kicking   123
   Propelling the Ball by Hand   125
      The Underhanded Throw   125
      The Overhand Throw   125
      The Overhanded Two-Handed Throw   125
   Defending Against Two Players on a Breakaway 126

6. Drills   127

Homework   127
  Trapping and Kicking   127
  Volleying   128
  Dribbling   128
    Dribble and Run   129
    Sensitivity of Touch   129
    Jump and Ball Bounce   129
    Rolling Ball   130
  Practicing with the Ball Rebound Board 131
At Practice   132
  Keeping the Players' Attention   132
  Trapping Drills   133
    Basic Trapping   133
    Trapping and Shielding   134
    Chest Trapping   135
    Body Trapping   135
  Dribbling   136
  Shoulder Charging   136
  Dribbling Feint   137
  Once-On   139
    Rolling Ball   139
    Rolling Ball with Teammate, Variation 1   140
    Rolling Ball with Teammate, Variation 2   140
    Heading   141
  Trap and Shooting   142
    Variation 1   142
    Variation 2   142
    Variation 3   142
  Other Scoring Drills   142
    Variation 1   142
    Variation 2   143
    Variation 3   143
  Crossing Drills   143
    The Blind Cross   143
    The Nonblind Cross   144
  Wall Passing   145
  Shielding   146

Defensive Drill 148
Two Against the Goalkeeper Drill 149
Throw-in Drills 149
    Variation 1 149
    Variation 2 150
Substitution of Advanced Techniques into Drills 150
Waste-of-Time Drills 150

7. Advanced Techniques for Field Players 153

Kicks 154
    Outside-of-the-Foot Kick 154
    More About the Angled Instep Kick 155
    Duck-Bill Instep Kick 156
    Under-the-Body Instep Kick 156
    Front-Volley and Half-Volley Kicks 158
    Side-Volley Kick 159
    Scissors Kick 160
    Blind-Cross Kick 160
    Back-Heel Kick 163
    Instep-Stride Shot 163
    Toe Poke 164
    Chip Kick 165
Traps 165
    More About the Inside-of-the-Foot Trap 165
    Under-the-Foot Trap 167
    Head Traps 167
    Side-of-the-Thigh Trap 168
    Top-of-the-Thigh Trap 169
    Calf Trap 169
    Outside-of-the-Foot Trap 170
    Dropping-Ball Trap 170
    Pseudo Trap 171
Tackles 172
    Standing-Block Tackle 172
    Sliding Tackle 173
    Sliding-Block Tackle 174
    Shoulder-Charge Tackle 176
    Two-Person Tackle 176

Appendix: Laws of the Game   179

I.	The Field of Play	179
II.	The Ball	181
III.	Number of Players	181
IV.	Players' Equipment	182
V.	Referees	183
VI.	Linesmen	184
VII.	Duration of the Game	184
VIII.	The Start of Play	185
IX.	Ball In and Out of Play	186
X.	Method of Scoring	186
XI.	Off-Side	186
XII.	Fouls and Misconduct	187
XIII.	Free-Kick	189
XIV.	Penalty Kick	190
XV.	Throw-In	191
XVI.	Goal-Kick	192
XVII.	Corner Kick	192

Index   195

Listing of Drawings, Photographs and Form

Drawings
- 3-1   The inside-of-the-foot trap.
- 3-2   Heading.
- 3-3   Shielding immediately upon receiving the ball.
- 3-4   Moving with a shielded ball.
- 3-5   Turning with the ball.
- 3-6   Shielding while turning.
- 3-7   Shielding against the touch line.
- 3-8   Correct defensive posture.
- 3-9   The body trap.
- 3-10 The instep kick.
- 3-11 The in-swinger vs. the out-swinger kick.
- 3-12 The inside-of-the-foot pass.
- 3-13 Chest trapping.
- 3-14 Throw-ins.
- 4-1   The W-M formation.
- 4-2   The 4-3-3 formation.
- 4-3   An ideal attack.
- 4-4   Direct shots taken from small angles.
- 4-5   The wall pass against one defender.
- 4-6   Setting up walls.
- 4-7   Setting up the penalty kick.
- 5-1   The goalkeeper's correct caught ball protection.
- 5-2   The goalkeeper's stance.
- 5-3   The goalkeeper remaining stationary during a breakaway by an opposing player.

5-4   Defensive setup against a corner kick.
5-5   Punching the ball out safely.
5-6   Tipping the ball over the net.
5-7   Catching low balls.
5-8   Diving practice.
5-9   The initial positions for the punt and the final punt.
6-1   The sensitivity of touch drill.
6-2   The contact points on the feet for the jump and ball-bounce drill.
6-3   The rolling ball drill.
6-4   The specifications for the ball rebound board.
6-5   The basic trapping drill.
6-6   The line-up for the feint drill.
6-7   Once-on shots on goal drill.
6-8   The heading once-on drill lineup.
6-9   The blind cross air ball lineup.
6-10 The nonblind cross drill lineup.
6-11 The wall pass drill lineup.
6-12 The monkey-in-the-middle drill lineup.
6-13 The throw-in drill lineup.
7-1   The outside-of-the-foot kick.
7-2   The under-the-body-instep kick.
7-3   The front-volley and half-volley kicks.
7-4   The side-volley kick.
7-5   The wrong and correct cross.
7-6   The blind-cross kick.
7-7   The toe poke.
7-8   The contact point of the foot with the dropping ball trap.
7-9   Trapping high balls that are passing the player to either right or left side.
7-10 The under-the-foot trap.
7-11 The head trap.
7-12 The side-of-the-thigh trap.
7-13 The top-of-the-thigh trap.
7-14 The calf trap.
7-15 The outside-of-the-foot trap.
7-16 The dropping-ball trap.
7-17 The standing-block tackle.

7-18 The sliding tackle.

7-19 The sliding-block tackle.

7-20 The shoulder-charge tackle.

Photographs

1　Dribbling the ball near the feet.

2　Shielding in action.

3　The final stages of the full-body-coordinated punt.

4　The goal kick.

5　The outside-of-the-foot kick.

Introduction

Youth soccer, a major sport throughout most of the world, is now growing at a phenomenal rate in North America. This book came about from personal experiences and observations and is aimed at presenting the total scene of youth soccer. Since 1975, I have been intensely involved in soccer as a manager, player, coach and referee and in other capacities.

My coaching experience has revolved around boys and girls from seven years old to adults. From this diversified experience, I have learned that winning games and championships comes about by building teams around players who develop self-discipline, ball control skills, and a strong defense. It is vital that a good offense be centered around a solid defense.

During my coaching years, one of my main objectives was to learn as much as possible about this fascinating sport in order to increase my own knowledge of it and to pass it on to my three sons. I believe that I was successful here. All three were among the top soccer players in their high school leagues and also in Rhode Island. One became a first-team, all-state goalkeeper with a full college scholarship.

It is unfortunate that many potentially talented young players play on teams with coaches who only want immediate wins; these players never get the technical training needed for their later years when the competition gets tough. Some coaches only think about winning the next game instead of developing the players to their full potential. "Ball control" is the name of today's soccer game and this is how this game should be promoted.

As can be seen by watching the better teams in first class soccer, these players employ ball control. It is important that young players understand that if they wish to have a future in this sport, they too must develop ball control and self-control. Today the best teams are playing "short-ball" soccer. In short-ball soccer, the ball is kept on the ground most of the time. To accomplish this, short passes are made to close players who trap the ball at their feet and protect it by shielding it with their body from opponents. "Long-ball" soccer is becoming a game of the past. This type of soccer uses long passes to front-line attacking players. Unfortunately, these forward players seldom get sufficient control of the ball to make effective shots on goal. It is usually the opposition defense people who end up with the ball, but then they too send the ball up to their forwards, where it is again intercepted. This type of soccer often resembles a tennis match in which the spectators all look up field in one direction and then down in the other direction every few seconds. This style of soccer play is not enjoyable to watch.

This book is intended to present an overview of highly skillful modern soccer and to elaborate on most of the skills and tactics necessary to reach this end. In order for North American teams to be capable of competing anywhere, their leagues must produce players who come up to par with countries that have been continuously supplying most of today's competitive skillful players.

The interested parent should have an overview of soccer because they either chose this sport for their child or they allowed the child to choose it. The choice is an excellent one because it requires the development of stamina and the mastery of many body skills, and it can include a good gender mixture and can develop some useful leadership skills. To be excellent in soccer, self-control, much self-practice, and the desire to attain an array of skills is required. To develop leadership qualities, self-confidence is a requirement. It is incumbent on the parent to oversee the child in this activity. And if your child gets on a team whose coach is unfair, is interested only in winning, and has no true comprehension of the modern version of this sport, you should consider some alternatives discussed in Chapter 1. It is in your child's best interest to have good coaches if he is to develop into a skillful player. If this eventually does occur, it is important that the child remain objective and become a strong team player because this is a team sport that wins games through the team. This child should also be instructed to develop humility because without this quality, others will strongly resist his leadership. A good leader can demonstrate excellent technical skills, can communicate well with others, and remain humble (not meek).

It is important not to dwell on the negative, but without some of the coaching negatives being explored, the positive factors will require longer learning times. As an example, I would like to state that I have seen many talented, potentially good soccer players have short careers because coaches reward these players for unskillful activities on the field. Some examples of these activities are not passing the ball to unmarked teammates while trying to be "the whole team," making long, wild kicks on goal, not trapping the ball, and making too many "once-on" kicks. When these players compete at the next level, experienced coaches will usually not be interested in them. On the other hand, coaches unfortunately sometimes chastise young players who make mistakes while they are endeavoring to apply the skills taught in practices.

Learning is by positive reinforcement and repetition. This book has been designed around this principle. It is about the analysis of skills, tactics, leadership, players, and game assessment. It is also about strategy — to put the player, coach, manager, referee, and the parent in control through an understanding of modern soccer. It is not only about developing winning players and winning games, but also about related and required self-control, effective soccer skill teaching, leadership on the field, skillful play, tactics, and the fairness expected by almost everyone interested in this sport.

1. Getting Started

To understand soccer and to know how to win games, it is necessary to have an understanding of all facets of this sport. It is my opinion that in North America, where this sport is gaining a strong foothold, it is frequently not very well understood. Often it is erroneously perceived to be an uncomplicated game. At one time it was, but with the development of modern ground ball soccer, the game may be considered to fall into two categories: the mostly outdated "long-ball" game and the modern "short-ball" game. In "long-ball" soccer (frequently a game of kickball), the ball is often kicked or headed up-field indiscriminately. The ball changes teams very frequently. The "short-ball" game is performed with strong defenses and with all players making accurate, short passes to teammates in any field direction. The intent is to maintain possession of the ball while waiting for opposition defensive mistakes, thus gaining the best opportunities for attacks on the opposition goal.

This book is designed to instruct entry-level as well as experienced people about all of the aspects of soccer that are necessary for developing a sound foundation for successful players' careers in this sport. This foundation is attained through the practices of ball control and basic techniques; later more advanced techniques can be developed. This book is intended to be both an elementary and advanced reference handbook. These basic techniques are the building blocks that are required to enable those players who fully or even partially master them to have a place in this sport for many future years. Just how far these players go depends upon several factors such as (1) being able to control the ball, (2) developing self-confidence through ball control and self-control, (3) love and understanding of the sport, (4) the parents' encouragement, (5) the ability to accept constructive criticism, (6) the ability to learn from both good and bad experiences, (7) good coaches who not only teach all players, but also give individual attention, and (8) parents who see that the child does not remain on a team that has an indifferent coach who may destroy that child's athletic confidence for his lifetime.

If the child has a strong desire to quit his team, the coach is probably not giving that child sufficient playing time in games. If the child plays on a house league team, there is probably a rule requiring that each player is to play at least one-half of each game. If you are a parent of a child on a team that has this rule and it is being overridden by the coach, you should bring this to the attention of the league at the next meeting. You as a parent should provide guidance by developing an interest in the child's training. Whether or not your child has a gift in this sport, he will benefit greatly if you become involved and develop an overall understanding of this sport to monitor his progression throughout the years.

What Is Soccer About?

Soccer is known as a noncontact sport. This is not quite true, as contact is frequent. It is generally not a heavy contact sport, however. Light shoulder charging and body pushing (under certain circumstances) are legal tactics. Body pushing is permitted when an opposing player purposely obstructs (screens) a player from access to the ball. Heavy contact is illegal, but it does occur. If it is observed and the laws are enforced by the referee, a penalty will result.

As stated previously, soccer has become a complex sport as a result of the many skills that are required to be a skillful player. Nearly all players lack some of the skills, but the better ones master thirty or forty skills. (Many must be learned with both the right and the left legs and feet.) Soccer players must make decisions quickly, and the advanced players mentally prepare their moves prior to contacting the ball. That is, they think about what will be the most advantageous move to make should they come in contact with the ball. It is also advantageous to verbally assist teammates (quietly) who may not see an oncoming opposing player. While there are many skills needed for the advanced player, these are not necessary for the beginning players.

Some of the advanced skills for the ten field players are as follows (many should be performed on both sides of the body):

1. Trapping with the inner part of the foot (near the ankle)
2. Trapping with the outer part of the foot (the top of the toes)
3. Trapping under the sole of the foot
4. Trapping with the thigh (top and side)
5. Trapping with the chest and body (several types)
6. Trapping with the head
7. Shielding (two types: when first contacting the ball and after possession of the ball)
8. Kicks with as least four parts of the foot: with the area just below the ankle for a push pass, with the instep, with the top of the four smaller toes, and with the big toe for a toe poke
9. Kicks that are meant to be high or low
10. Head passes
11. Dribbling (many types, dependent on the situation)
12. Crossing, passing, back-heel passes, when to pass or when not to pass
13. How to defend properly
14. How to draw off players
15. Throw-ins
16. How to score
17. Volleying (front and side)
18. Tackling
19. Learning the laws of the game

In addition to the individual skills (there are more than those listed), players must be taught that they are not the focal point of the team; the team only wins tough games that are played as a team. Therefore each player with the ball should, most of the time, be unselfishly looking for opportunities that involve teammates. When a player is without the ball on offense, he must constantly be going into open spaces to receive potential passes or to lure away opponents.

The above discussion of skills mainly involves the ten field players. The goalkeeper must eventually master many catching, diving, pushing, and punching ball defensive techniques. Offensively, his role is also vital to the team's performance but this role is often misunderstood and therefore played to a minimum. This player needs to gain self-confidence to utilize many verbal commands and develop into a team leader who can play the most important role on the team: taking full charge of the defense.

If you are an entry-level coach or parent, you should be aware of the complex nature of the skills that will be observed in highly skilled games seen at the college or professional level. What you will be seeing at the highest level of play is ball control and self-control. But at young-age levels, very few skills will be commonly exercised except by a few exceptional individuals. Playing the modern "short-ball soccer" (generally an on-the-ground passing game), young players must use parts of the body they are unaccustomed to use for ball control. It is especially difficult for them because of the approaching speed of opponents and their limited mobility in a crowded space. With the very young, games are played on smaller fields, and thus their space is even further limited.

A primary objective for a potentially good coach is to understand the problems of the players from an overall standpoint. Skillful play is difficult when there is opponent pressure, but this quality of play should be an objective. Insisting that the players stick with the basic ball control skills when one is coaching these skills at practice will instill some respect from the players. Allowing unskilled playing in scrimmage games to continue after the players have been taught proper methods is counter productive. Also, it may be your desire to promote skillful activities, but sharing team responsibilities with another may cause conflicts. If you are co-coaching or managing a team with a veteran player, he may only desire to have immediate wins and have a complete disregard for promoting basic skills. This is definitely a difficult situation. It is best to agree upon each coach's duties and training objectives beforehand to remove future disagreements. If this is not arranged on a permanent basis, much of the coaching enjoyment will be reduced because disagreements will be unavoidable. If you are just an interested parent and observe activities that are in your view counterproductive, you should make your views known at league meetings.

To improve your own powers of observation, try to get an overall understanding of skillful game play by observing high quality games. Notice that the ball is usually on the ground and there is prolonged possession of the ball by each team. In poor games, observe the lack of ball control, the poor officiating, and generally uncontrolled activities. Whether or not you have soccer experience, get involved with the team's training and practice games and play in scrimmage games as a goalkeeper or defender; do not be concerned about looking "bad." Practice the homework drills outlined in the book. All coaches and future coaches could benefit from some additional practice that would help them comprehend modern soccer better.

Leadership

Soccer is a natural sport for mixed teams. It brings both genders closer together for a common soccer cause. This fosters leadership. It seems that girls stay on mixed teams longer in soccer than in other sports, allowing more functional interactions and communication between the sexes. Historically, it is quite apparent that sport has evolved from very early times from a form of combat or defense, and it is traditionally the older males that pass on their skills to the young males. At the present time, most of the sport's skills and knowledge are with the males. Today, however, there are many girls playing in mixed gender soccer. As the girls get older, many will switch to all-girls teams. They will carry with them the idea of leadership they picked up from the coaches who taught them the sport. They will now possess either good or bad leadership skills based on their experience. If the coaches are aware of the image that they present to others, they would be careful to present a good one by having self-control, by being consistent in following through on statements, and by showing a sense of fairness.

The girls also add to the mix, the element that boys need — maturity — because girls are more mature in general. With the girls around, boys and men are more apt to use self-control and to have more self-awareness. This may seem a minor issue, but in reality, leadership has two main ingredients. Those ingredients are self-awareness and self-control.

When people get angry, they are out of control. Anger occurs fairly often on the soccer field. When a child sees an adult get outraged, that child may think that anger can be appropriate; but, it has no place in soccer. When a person is angry, that person is out of control. Anger usually occurs on the soccer field because of poor and biased officiation involving issues such as unpenalized violence. It also may occur when a player is penalized for exercising a legal tactic such as shoulder charging or when a player bumps another because the opponent was illegally screening the ball. Referees themselves are leaders. They are good leaders when they fully know the laws of the game and fairly control the game. Poor refereeing should not be acceptable; leagues should pay more attention to officiation. There should be a referees' trainer and a referees' coordinator. The referees' coordinator job is discussed in the next section. Discipline of poor officials is a necessary function of the league. If the league is willing to pay higher fees to referees, it will attract better quality officials. With less anger on the playing fields, the players can concentrate on the game and the skills. Also, coaches who have only one objective — to win — are not doing the league or the players a service. They should also be disciplined even though they are "badly needed." When the league does not discipline itself, the sport's objectives are compromised. Leagues that exercise fairness are healthy ones exhibiting good league leadership.

Negative leadership is encouraged by some coaches who acquire little or no knowledge of what this sport is all about. Getting the ball through the opponent's goal as many times as possible may seem central to entry-level soccer, but one would hope that as one goes up in level, the coach learns that skills are required to counteract the defensive play of skillful opponents. With a lack of this knowledge, they negate their training by shouting contradictions or meaningless statements such as "get the ball," "kick it," "burn him," "good kick," or "good try" (when it was not a good try).

There is a correct situation for trapping the ball or not trapping it, for dribbling or passing, etc. These situations become known to players when they are allowed to experiment with the knowledge learned in the drills. They must be allowed to make mistakes using their newly acquired training knowledge (on valid tries) and not be chastised because they tried to trap the ball or tried to dribble. On the other hand, "star players" often are not chastised when their play is self-serving.

One of the worst examples of negative leadership is telling players that they will not play in games if they do not appear in practices. It is the rule rather than the exception that coaches who make this statement do not keep their word on this issue. Those poorer athletes who come to every practice often sit out much of the game while a "star" player who missed many practices plays the whole game. If you as a coach are going to play these better athletes to the maximum, it is best not to make any statements regarding showing up for practices.

As a good coach, maintain consistency, allow the players to experiment with the tactics you taught them, and maintain self-control at all times. Find channels to report unfair practices and possibly set up formal methods to air complaints and formulate solutions to these complaints.

Coach Development

Coaches entering youth soccer come from a variety of soccer backgrounds. Many have had no soccer background to speak of, but are parents who want to get involved. Whatever the background, most coaches are inexperienced in handling up to 18 players for 11 different positions. Even with experience, viewing the team as a whole is very different from having played just a few positions. Nevertheless, I have known many soccer coaches without playing experience who have been successful.

An inexperienced coach can begin by familiarizing himself with the objectives of a good soccer coach (besides winning the next game). Then he can segment the team for general defense and general attack. It is also imperative that he watch top-class indoor and outdoor soccer on TV or live. It is important to be able to discern the difference between good and poor quality soccer. One useful method for determining soccer quality is to observe the negative aspects of the game.

Coaches who have experience in soccer have an initial obvious advantage over inexperienced coaches. This experience may, however, actually act as a hindrance to learning about the game from a coach's standpoint. There can be 18 players to manage instead of just oneself. The experience may also prevent a coach from accepting modern soccer if she was not well trained in this discipline. Modern soccer, as stated before, is played by maintaining possession of the ball with short no-risk passes as frequently as possible. Long-ball soccer is for the most part outdated in the better leagues. It is a game in which the ball is kicked or headed down field to attacking players. Unfortunately, they usually do not receive the ball, or when they do, they often do not maintain control of it for constructive purposes.

As mentioned earlier, all coaches (including nonskilled coaches and potential ones) are encouraged to participate in practice games. A new coach could start out as one of the goalkeepers or a wing defender. As a goalkeeper, assure that each of your defenders is keeping an eye on the opponent in his territory. Do not try to catch most of the balls at the end of your reach; instead, tip them away safely. As a defender, never forget this rule: always stay goalside of your opponent in your territory. This means always place yourself between the ball and the goal and always watch the opponent in your territory. Also keep your legs closed up to prevent a pass from going under you. Do not try to dislodge the ball from the opponent unless she loses its control. These topics are further discussed in the goaltending and defensive sections in the book. Jogging and running are also strongly suggested. Get involved with the homework drills and possibly build a body rebound board shown in Chapter 6 to practice heading with your eyes open.

Poor Quality Play

The following information should enable anyone to distinguish between good and poor quality soccer (poor quality being a game of kickball).

1. If the ball goes over the touch line (sideline) in outdoor soccer and indoor soccer with sidelines more than once every minute, the game is poor; more than once every five minutes, the game is of medium quality. It is a high quality game when the ball almost never goes over the touch line.

2. If the ball is placed into the air and kept up three or four times in succession without being settled and controlled on the ground by one or both of the teams, and this happens continuously throughout

the game, the game is of poor quality. If this happens once in five minutes, the game is medium quality. If the ball is almost continuously kept on the ground and both teams pass it around at least four or five times to themselves, it is a high quality game.

3. If players are constantly getting injured or the referee stops the play every one or two minutes for a penalty, the game is of poor quality. Also, if the referee does not stop the game when there are continuous rule infractions, the game is of poor quality. If these problems occur less frequently, the game is of medium quality. If very few infractions occur, say in ten minutes of play, the referees have excellent control of the game and it is probably a high quality game.

4. If five or more players usually converge on the ball in front of the goal, the game is poor quality.

These negative aspects of soccer are pointed out to show coaches what to look out for in their own games. These negative aspects will generally occur whenever the people who are involved are out of control. Coaches who have an interest in high quality soccer should work towards the positive aspects of soccer. The more that the sport is understood, the more control will be placed in the areas of coaching the players and refereeing.

Important Areas of Control

1. Control of Officials. It is up to each parent and coach to insure that the league has the highest level of referees possible. Often teenage players are chosen to referee younger age group games. They usually miss calling many fouls because of their inexperience. Along with your league's referee coordinator (a person linking the league president and the head referee), there should be a referee trainer. This person's job is very important to the league, but is often overlooked as being not worth the time and effort. As a new coach, if you find that your league does not have a referee's trainer, you should bring this to the attention of the league officers at meetings. This individual's job is an ongoing job of continuously updating the referee's knowledge of the game. If the matter is brushed aside, everyone involved will eventually pay the price because referees will call legal tactics fouls and will

overlook many fouls, some of them serious ones. In some instances, frustrated coaches who have taught perfectly legal, but less familiar, skills may tell players to stop employing them because they fear a player will be ejected from the game. If the league is interested in developing the highest standards, it will pay attention to this very important aspect of the game.

2. Ball Control. This is what every team should strive for. The ball is more manageable on the ground because it only has to be maneuvered in a single plane. This type of soccer enables the players to have better control and to maintain possession longer. Maintaining possession longer is the object of modern soccer because it enables the team to take clearer and better directed shots on goal instead of taking too many wild and wasted "once-on" shots on goal in a kickball match. For example, a short ground pass to a player 10' (3 meters) to 15' (4 1/2 meters) away can take three seconds to settle, but it takes about eight seconds to settle an air ball going the same distance. I have demonstrated this in practices every season, but it sometimes takes a few attempts to make an effective demonstration and to prove the point.

Ball control starts with trapping to settle the ball. Doing this under pressure requires an accompanying move called shielding. It is the most basic skill needed for ball control. It is strongly recommended that this single most important skill be encouraged and mastered by all players, including the goalkeeper, who will at times dribble the ball outside the penalty area. If the concept of shielding is not clear, use the analogy of this tactic in basketball. Shielding is done naturally in basketball after the player starts moving and dribbling: basketball players always shield the ball with their back to the opponent who is nearby. In soccer there is one basic difference, however. Shielding is necessary at the time of trapping. The types of shielding are discussed in Chapter 3.

3. Coach Control. This section mainly applies to coaches, but it also applies to parents. It is important to remain calm and maintain self-control at an amateur soccer match. If you remain calm or even smile when a nonpenalized infraction occurs, referees and others will often take notice of your attitude and may even try to come up to your level. This is important for you because while the players are being taught soccer, you are advancing your leadership qualities.

Coaches who see repeated infractions committed against their team that are not penalized by one of the officials may get angry. It is very difficult to remain calm under such circumstances, but an attempt must be made at self-control. It is better to gently call out the observed infraction to the referee, calmly stating, for example, "handball ref." The same low voice can be used to correct players who are not performing as instructed in practices, using statements such as: "John, you were told to stay goalside of your man and not go for the ball, be more careful next time." This of course must only be done in lower level leagues where coaching from the side lines is permitted. Anger does not resolve any problem, although some people think there is a place for it. If you have a complaint, and there is no formal complaint system in effect, report the incident at a league meeting, giving the name of the individual causing the problem. This complaint should be made by parents and coaches. If decisions are unjustly made to accommodate some "needed" coach or referee, the situation will not improve. If no satisfaction is given to you and the situation worsens, it is time to move on to another league, possibly in another town. Even if you are not a coach, but a parent, it is advisable to place your child in another (different) town league. In either case, you may have to volunteer your time for a job in the new league. While I believe that most leagues make an honest attempt to remain fair, I have known some leagues or coaches that did not have the players' interests at heart.

4. Player Control. If the game is under control, with older teams, there should be two players controlling the field action of the other players. These players are the goalkeeper and the center half back (providing that the formation requires a center half back). In the child's earlier years of play, however, these players will not be in control of the defense. Nevertheless, leadership can be encouraged, and these players should be taught to have some responsibility for the others' activities on the field.

If the above controls are being implemented, then there should be a sufficient setting for good soccer contests. It sometimes happens, however, that a team that may be accustomed to winning is now losing because its players are outskilled. Because of their frustrations, they may start playing "dirty." These players and their coach are out of control, and good referees will not permit this situation to exist. If the referees do not take control of the situation, however, there is little that can be done at the time except possibly to leave the field and file a formal complaint with the league. To be in control, you must decide your priorities. I have personally stopped games (as the head referee) and reprimanded the offending team's coaches, telling them that the game will be terminated if the roughness does not cease.

Substitute Players

A soccer team has up to 18 players, with 11 on the playing field during game play. That means that up to 7 players are waiting on the side lines. In outdoor soccer, as stated above, house leagues generally have a rule allowing each child to play one-half of each game. As an interested parent, assure that coaches abide by this rule. Placing the weaker players on the field for five minutes at a time and playing them for an accumulated time that is slightly less than half of the game does not actually fulfill each child's right to play in half of the game. A child learns almost nothing constructive by only playing in five minute bursts of time (in outdoor soccer). This mischievous substitution method should not be condoned. This does not apply, however, to indoor soccer because five minutes on the floor will fatigue nearly any player since there is no time to catch one's breath.

Coaches who are unfamiliar with soccer may apply substitution methods used in other sports. In football, substitutions may be made by placing a new line of players on the field. This does not work in soccer because a player must generally take several minutes to get into the tempo of the game. Also, changes are generally rather disruptive, especially when they are frequent. It is best not to substitute a particular player more frequently than in one-quarter blocks. Not only are frequent substitutions disruptive to the team, they are also nerve-racking to the coach. This is especially true when young players are constantly asking the coach "when can I go in?" Coaches may consider the following solution for substitution to allow themselves more time to watch the game:

1. Prior to the game, a substitution plan can be written down. This plan gives each player the allotted time of play. Substitute the players into the game by the clock. Do not substitute the same player

more then three times. The plan should not use several weaker players in the game together. Spread them over the game and do not place them (when in at the same time) on the same side of the field. Instinctively, coaches like to use these weaker players in defense. This is not a good move: not scoring a goal is not the same as having one scored against you. Placing weaker players in the frontal attacking positions is the best option.

2. Appoint the assistant coach, manager, or a parent as the substitution coordinator. Substitutions cannot be made at any time, but only according to certain rules when the ball goes out of play. Typically, in outdoor soccer, substitutions are permitted when your team has a throw-in, during goal kicks by both sides, and when the clock is stopped for injuries. In youth soccer, these occurrences generally take place every few minutes. Naturally, deviations from the plan take place, but the plan works best when one adheres to it: this amounts to less stress on players, coaches, and parents. If you are a parent and your child is in a house league with the half-game rule for each child's playing time and your child is not getting proper play time, it is best to discuss this at league meetings. It is the exception to the rule that this problem can be straightened out directly with the coach. If you are not confident about getting a fair solution, remember that you have paid the entry fee for your child and also cite the written rule for playtime.

Can Parents Increase Their Child's Playing Time?

The question may arise as to why it is desirable to increase your child's playing time? It is desirable because you want your child to remain in the sport as long as possible to develop his confidence. There are obvious future benefits to scholastic and musical studies, but sport mastery has less obvious benefits. Having raised three sons in this sport (almost exclusively in soccer), I can associate these related beneficial results to their present-day lives. They have self-confidence, they do not use any harmful substances, and they are used to working hard to attain their goals and desires.

Very often it can be observed that a child will play a different sport before or after going to soccer practice. This is not recommended. Soccer is difficult to master and even more difficult to learn when it is competing with another sport. During soccer season, "pickup" games in other sports should be discouraged. By applying the soccer principles learned at practice to playing in "pick-up" soccer games, the child will eventually outclass other children who do not take the sport seriously. So one sport should be encouraged, and a variety of simultaneous sports should be discouraged. It is not easy to learn something well, and one can do so only by the constant repetition derived from focusing on only one activity at a time. And it is rare that any child will become highly competitive in more then one sport.

The following information should probably be in a text on child psychology, but I believe it is pertinent here. As a parent, I think I am qualified to state this observation. I have often observed that only one of two children (generally of the same sex) who are close in age in a family seems to be the natural athlete and the other seems to have no athletic inclination. From observation, I see this to be the result of parental attitudes towards these children. The favored child is usually encouraged by adults. The favored child also often has the seemly unrelated characteristic that she knowingly provokes the other child only while not in view of adults. Then the other child retaliates, but often in the view of these same adults. The result is that an unfair judgment is made about the child who is not favored. This child develops little self-confidence, while the "protected" child actually develops a false sense of self-confidence. This excessive and deficient self-confidence is then carried over into sports. It is beneficial for both children for the parent to be aware of this situation and to encourage both equally. This will help develop true self-confidence that is necessary for advanced competition.

It is recommended that you as a parent observe your child's soccer practices and go to games. You may be surprised at what you can learn. You may observe some undesirable characteristics that have thus far escaped your observation. By learning about these, you may prudently take corrective measures to encourage correct behavior before the child grows up. In my opinion, one of the worst characteristics that an athlete can have is to be "noncoachable," to be unable to take corrective criticism. If this characteristic is observed, it is beneficial to the child to be instructed that corrective criticism is not to be confused with criticism.

A child on the verge of quitting soccer is probably a noncompetitive athlete or does not like the coach. In this situation, the coach often wants to have as little to do with this child as possible. While there is something to be said for allowing the child to quit, it may be better to encourage the child to remain on the team as long as possible, unless you think that the coach should not be coaching children. Allowing the child to immediately quit may encourage quitting something simply because of laziness. If the child blames others for his failures, bitterness is the result. There is a useful expression: "Don't get bitter, just better." It is really in the child's best interest to remain on the team and improve by receiving encouragement and by practicing the homework drills. But immediate recognition by any coach is not likely to occur. The child may have a long way to go to become competitive.

Get involved and learn the game. As a parent and possibly the child's coach, get personally involved with your child and spend several minutes a week alone with him on a particular skill. It may be throwing the ball for heading and observing whether the child keeps his eyes open and whether the ball is making contact with the correct part of the head. It may be to find a lawn, field, or street where you can kick and dead-trap fast balls back to each other: trapping the balls dead at the feet is a must. Keeping the eye on the ball is also a must. It may be throwing the ball for tipping practice if your child is a goalkeeper. Pick any one skill and work with him and continue with this drill until it is successfully used in games.

One of the most common mistakes that many parents and some coaches make is to assume that the child is correctly performing a certain skill. An adult may often be afraid to challenge the child because of fear of intimidation. It may be assumed that the child has properly learned some task or skill. After you correctly learn about the skill, insist that the child perform it correctly. Unfortunately, a few coaches may not know how to perform certain skills and may be demonstrating them wrongly. You should only work with those skills that you are certain you understand. The basics are in this book; you can teach them effectively.

A parent can increase the child's playing time anywhere from a small increment to a large increment depending upon the personal effort expended. Using the same approach that is used for studying school work or learning a musical instrument — constant insistence on doing the homework drills — will have a positive effect.

Aggression and Roughness

Aggressiveness in sport should not be confused with acts of violence. Aggressiveness for the ten field players in soccer is the spirit for winning a "loose ball" (a ball not in possession of either team). An aggressive player tries to get to the ball first, shielding while trapping the ball, defends when the team is not in possession of the ball, and draws opponents away from a teammate who is dribbling the ball. An aggressive goalkeeper punches a ball out of a crowded goal area, quickly throws the ball to a teammate, commands respect from her defenders, and forcibly shouts "keeper" when she wants the ball.

When the playing starts to get rough and dirty, the line has been crossed from legal aggressiveness to violence. When a defender pulls the shirt of an attacking player or trips a player who has just dribbled the ball past him, the playing is getting rough and illegal. If such playing is not curtailed by the referees, it worsens. Players may try to hurt the goalkeeper, so they must learn ways to defend themselves. It is up to the referees to observe hostile situations and take proper measures to bring order to the playing field.

It is worth comparing aggression occurring with children in middle-class areas with that occurring with children from poorer areas. I have often observed that the children from poorer areas are more aggressive on the field and that middle-class children may be intimidated by them. There is a drill that equalizes this aggression and teaches legal aggressiveness and the amount of roughness permitted by the laws of soccer. This is the shoulder charging drill in Chapter 6.

An excellent soccer player has creative intelligence and curiosity for learning, develops endurance, develops skills, improves her speed, learns all of the aspects of the game, and is aggressive on the field. Many highly skillful players have all the above ingredients but lack aggressiveness. When matched up against aggressive unskillful players, they are often intimidated. Therefore it is necessary to teach players the amount of aggressiveness and roughness that is legally permitted by the laws of soccer. An example from my own experience is relevant. I was a manager-coach of a men's ethnic soccer team. These players all had excellent skills brought over from the "old country." During the first four games, we were two or three goals up on our opponents. As each game progressed, however, the "home grown" team learned that they could intimidate our players by excessive roughness. We lost all four games. I then decided to teach each one of my players my shoulder charging drill. I personally worked with each and every player to instill into him this skill that he was unaware of. From that point on, we won every game and went on to win the season's championship. Possibly the players would have won anyway without my coaching, but I like to think that the shoulder charging exercise had something to do with our victories.

Conditioning and Injuries

Soccer is a sport that requires a large amount of energy and power. Energy is necessary for players to have endurance for staying competitive in the game until its end. Power is needed for large bursts of energy that are required in a small time frame when accelerating or running at top speed. The training at soccer practices strives to build up each player's endurance limits to meet the rigorous requirements demanded of a soccer player; much of this training must be done in the early part of each season prior to the commencement of official games.

Players must be able to run backwards as well as forward for the time that they are out on the playing field, so the run training should include backwards running. During the game there is little time to rest. In indoor soccer, the ability to stay in the game is even harder to attain because there are virtually none of the resting periods that may occur briefly during outdoor matches. The athletes who have the most stamina are those who run and exercise on their own time, especially before the training season begins. A prudent coach will instruct her players to start with self-disciplined preseason conditioning that includes running and stretching activities.

A very important part of the soccer player's supervised training is stretching and warm-up drills prior to the commencement of soccer drills and games. If these stretching and warm-up drills are not taken seriously, some players will probably experience torn muscles on the top of the thigh (the quadratus femoris — the kicking muscle), on the thigh near the groin (the iliacus, psoas, and abductors), or on the back of the lower calf (the gastrocnemius). Some of the players may also sprain their ankles or develop knee problems. A set of stretching and warm-up exercises should be put together by the coach under the supervision of a qualified medical person to help the team stay fit and to help prevent muscle and joint injuries. It is also highly recommended that each player consult a physician prior to the initiation of any strenuous exercise program.

Equipment

Each player should own a good quality soccer ball and bring it to practice. A good quality ball probably starts at the moderate price range. Buying the lowest price soccer ball may not be economical in the long run because these balls just do not hold up under the abusive treatment given to them by constant kicking. In addition, certain low-quality balls can be painful when headed and they may not bounce correctly, especially if the ball is out of balance or becomes so.

If a player purchases an expensive ball, she must watch it carefully. Other people may take notice of it, especially at an "away" soccer field. Coaches, too, are to be advised that when they are supplying the game ball, they must retrieve it immediately after the match. During games, if possible, keep all extra balls in a ball bag and keep track of any training balls that are outside of the ball bag. Also, be aware of this common trick that can be employed to remove a soccer ball from your possession: two children may start kicking a ball around and then kick it over a fence or into a grassy or wooded area. The ball is now out of sight to be retrieved later. Your soccer balls should also be indelibly marked with permanent ink for easy identification.

Each player will need some personal equipment. This personal equipment should include a cup and a good set of shin pads that also provide ankle protection. Warm, under-the-uniform garments are also suggested. Goalkeepers should also have goalie's gloves, knee, elbow, and hip pads. All players should also be requested to carry their own water to practices, preferably in quart- or liter-size containers.

Coaches should have at least three soccer balls and a ball bag. It is a good idea to have eight or ten field markers for drills and goalpost simulation. A first-aid kit containing the usual sport-emergency materials should be on hand at all times.

If oranges are to be supplied at games, there should be at least one for each player, and they should be thoroughly washed and cut into quarters. A parent should be designated to call a different family for each upcoming game to supply these oranges. There should also be a designated person to distribute these oranges evenly during the game. The coaches should not have to supply the oranges, nor have the task of assigning the player responsible for supplying them for each upcoming game. This job should be designated to a parent.

Clothing

It is important to know the weather prediction for the game. If it is going to be about 100°F (38°C), the game should perhaps be postponed. If the temperature is around 50°F (10°C) or less, each player should have a winter coat and the spectators should be aware that long johns will make the game more enjoyable, especially if it is windy.

Soccer fields can be very windy because they are a large, open space. Players and spectators usually underestimate how cold they will become during a game. The wind is a strong coolant. Players, especially young ones, should play in track suits or some suitable and acceptable long-sleeve and long-leg type of garments under their soccer uniform when the temperature is below 40°F (4°C) and even at higher temperatures if the wind chill factor is in this temperature range. Players may complain about this extra clothing, but without it they may be exposing themselves to hypothermia, a condition in which the body temperature falls a few degrees below normal. The result of being exposed to the elements such as rain, cold, and wind can lead to a cold or something more serious. This is especially true for the players sitting on the sidelines. Under these unfavorable climatic conditions, players sitting on the sidelines should always be directed to wear track suits, coats, or rain gear.

2. Skill Level

When a child is seven, eight, or nine years old, much time should be expended learning and reinforcing basic skills. During the games, skillful activity will not often be observed. As the children progress in age, skillful playing will be observed if their present and former coaches have been reinforcing the basics during games. It is a good idea for leagues to set training standards to which coaches are to adhere. To enforce these standards, it is important for the league to create a position of age group coordinator for each age group. This person's job would be to assure that all players in a particular age group be taught by drills in practice that are common to all players. This person need not be highly skillful in soccer but needs to observe that the prescribed drills are the same throughout all teams. If certain coaches do not conform to the league policies or know about certain skills, they should be required to attend a coaches' clinic run by an individual with soccer experience.

Very often coaches erroneously assume that the players have certain skills or will develop these skills as they grow older, but these skills are often not in place. If children are not taught the basic skills and these skills are not enforced, they will probably never develop them. All children in the youth program should have the same opportunities to learn the modern version of this sport (playing with skills), in the same way that all first grade children are taught to read at a prescribed level. You may not think that this is important if your child seems to be ahead of the others because he is scoring many goals. This may mean that your child is a "natural" at soccer, but this could also signify that the other players surrounding your child are poorly trained in defense. No child is a "natural" without the hard work of learning skills along with the development of self-control. You should also be concerned if the teams are kicking the ball uncontrollably up in the air most of the time. You may want to know if your child is just having recreation or if she is learning to play soccer skillfully. Observe the type of playing and ask at meetings why the ball is up in the air so often. If you get brushed off with an answer such as "the coaches are doing the best that they can," you are not getting a straight answer. Also ask if the coaches are coaching according to a league plan. If you do not get satisfactory answers here also, your child is probably in a kickball league. The point of this matter is not to make trouble for the league; it probably has enough problems. But you should still want your child's coach to teach and enforce basic skills. Make the league aware of your concern.

Advice for the Beginning Coach

The "beehive" formation is the type of style played by children when they are first introduced into soccer. At the starting line up, the half, or quarter, all players are ready in proper formation. After the start whistle is blown, all 20 field players immediately chase the ball. Just about everyone is out of the formation taught in practice, and the players immediately swarm after the ball, resembling bees around a beehive. When the ball gets kicked into the center of the beehive, all players who are near it try to kick it. When the ball pops out of the "hive," all 20 players follow it. This is normal at a young age and also comical. It is also natural for the frustrated coaches to constantly yell to the players to get into position, but at this age, they do not listen. To compound the problem, most spectators may be shouting to their sons and daughters: "kick it" and "that's the way." In time, this phase passes, and the players eventually do get the right idea. If you are a novice youth coach, you are going to experience many confusing days and nights both on and off the soccer field. It is advantageous to learn early, to accept the bad along with the good.

As players get older, extraordinary tension builds up at certain games, and it is a good idea to learn to observe all activities other than just those around the ball. To be a potentially good coach, you must remain rational and calm at all times even though you may be the only one on the field doing so. The questions that you might ask yourself at this time could be: Where are the other players? What is the other coach doing? What are the spectators doing? What is the referee doing? Perhaps the referees are making bad calls and the coaches and parents are screaming. The players may not be performing correctly, and up to seven players on the sidelines could be waiting impatiently to get into the game. If you look at this scene, you may wonder what you are doing here. It usually doesn't get any better, so the sooner that you get control of yourself and your team, the sooner you will realize that winning isn't the only reason that you are here. You have a job to do.

It is important to keep everything in prospective early in your coaching career. This is particularly important when everything seems to be out of control. Every coach that follows their children up through the years (and possibly all coaches) will have winning and losing teams throughout the years. You may lose a game more than once with a score of 16 to 0, and your own player may score the winning goal for the other team by kicking the ball in your own goal. It is most important to evaluate your coaching abilities by measuring the progress of players as they are learning to apply new skills. Some things are going to be out of your control. You may lose an important championship because of a biased or poor official or for other reasons. And be aware that whenever organizers develop fair rules for the best interests of everyone, there will be those mischievous individuals who find ways of "stacking" their team with preferred players, get certain favored referees for their games, etc. When you improve your self-control and learn to keep everything in proper prospective, you can see that you have gained something out of all of this experience. My best memories do not come from winning championships, but from the times when my teams ran circles around older and more experienced players and teams. These occurrences may have only lasted for ten minutes or so, but in looking back, the shock we gave to some of the opposing team coaches when this occurred was far better then winning.

Suggested Guidelines for Practices

By using practice drills that are meaningful for pressure game situations, you will be utilizing precious training time most efficiently.

It is very important to invest in the time for reiterating basic ball control, basic methods of defense, basic shooting-on-goal techniques, and proper basic goaltending techniques. When players develop and nurture these basics, they will grasp advanced techniques more readily. Especially in the players' younger years, some time should be devoted to assuring that these basic techniques have taken hold. Soccer practices usually occur two times per week for about two hours per practice. Some coaches give more time to practices, some give less time, but four hours a week is just about the minimum time a team should practice. Naturally, if a coach can devote more time to his team, the players will benefit from the training.

Many years ago when we were in the first year of our newly organized league, I saw an example of prolonged training. One of our traveling teams had lost a game by 15 to 0. Because our team was so grossly overpowered, I did some inquiring that day and had learned some remarkable facts. Very high winning scores for the opposing coach's team were typical. Spectators accompanying this team told me that the coach had been holding practices five times a week, and thus he had developed a powerful soccer machine. The players were not in themselves all that skillful, but the team moved like a powerhouse. Some people questioned the ethics of this man, especially when his final insult to us was a direct kick taken by his goalkeeper. And, yes, this player scored a goal. Whether this coach was doing the right thing for his players by overpowering soccer clubs is not important here, but it illustrates that with great effort, one can attain one's goals. His goal was to build a team that did not lose, and he apparently had the time to devote to this endeavor. I suppose that nearly all coaches would like to develop the winning team of their dreams, but most of them have only a limited time to train their team. This is why it is important to utilize time most efficiently and make training as close to actual game conditions as possible and to discard some common but inefficient drills, some of which are discussed in Chapter 6. It becomes obvious which drills are not useful when one gives thought to the applications.

For a normal practice schedule, it is good to start practices with a series of jogging exercises and then build up to running exercises. Be careful not to overdo it, especially when it is cold and muscles may be tight. Use good judgment about the number of laps that the players can safely do. Laps do not have to be done in succession, but one-fifth of each lap should be run backwards. Soccer players do need to run as frequently as possible, and they should be encouraged to do much of this on their own so they will not tire in games. More injuries occur when athletes are tired than when they are in good form. Players must be taught to run backwards. Since soccer players must "face the ball" when it is in possession of the opponents, running backwards as part of their normal training run is a good conditioner for them. The warm-up run is vital for the development of their "wind power" and their legs.

Their training should include stretching and warm-up exercises because they are essential to help prevent ankle and knee injuries and pulled muscles. Wind sprints should be performed from touch line to touch line. A time of about five to ten minutes should be spent explaining each drill and its application. This topic is further discussed in Chapter 6.

While it is preferable to demonstrate skill-related drills yourself, they can be performed by an older soccer player, a guest coach, or by your more experienced players. After the players have begun to practice the drills, it is important that they perform them correctly. If the exercises are being done incorrectly, recall the players and give them a further explanation. During these drills, do not allow them to get sloppy, to spread out too far, or to do any exercise not specified for that drill.

The most important drills are those that teach the basic skills. The basic skills are shielding, dribbling, trapping with the feet, heading, throw-ins, and two types of kicks. These kicks are the instep and the push pass kicks, as discussed in the next chapter.

The remainder of the practice should consist of a scrimmage game or games. With the little time available to scrimmage, it is advisable to have two simultaneous scrimmage games utilizing from four to five players per team. This way each player gets more time "on the ball." Use field markers for the goal posts. If there is a shortage of goalkeepers, close up the untended goal to about two feet wide. If there is only one goalkeeper available for each team, alternate her at midtime of this drill. Naturally, at the untended goal, goaltending is prohibited. An alternate method that utilizes only one goalkeeper is to play "half court" in the same manner as in basketball, where there are only two to four players per team. The rules are as follows: After receiving the ball for the first time (changing possession), that team must bring back the ball to a 10-yard (9-meter) line before it becomes eligible for a legal shot on goal. If a recovered or stolen ball is not brought back to the 10-yard (9-meter) line, it is offside and if a goal is scored, it does not count. The goalkeeper is on neither team and must throw the ball out to neutral ground.

The last twenty minutes of the practice should be spent on a full field while having a game with all players participating. This game should emphasize shielding, trapping, passing, and proper defense. If these skills are not utilized, the game should be interrupted as many times as necessary for an adequate explanation of where sloppy playing has occurred.

It is not recommended that "one-touch" or "two-touch" soccer be utilized at any time except for the "wall-pass" drill. This type of activity encourages players to kick the ball as soon as contact is made with it. In modern soccer, ball control is generally performed only when a player settles and shields the ball from opponents. The one- or two-touch method encourages players to think in the following manner: "I am not sure that I can trap the ball with this opponent bearing down on me, so I will not take a chance and settle it. If I lose it to the opponent, I will not look too good. So here Joe, you take it." One- or two- touch soccer is not applicable to ball control soccer.

Better Play and Team Work

It is suggested that the basic skills be drilled very frequently so that they will become spontaneous. More drills on personal skills can slowly be introduced, but it is not recommended until the players reach ten years of age. It should be the job of an age group coordinator to monitor practices to assure that coaches do not introduce advanced techniques prematurely. For example, teaching the use of the wall pass to young players will promote its excessive use and therefore reduce trapping and controlling the ball. Players need the self-confidence that they can trap a ball under pressure, protect it, and dribble it into open spaces. This is the mark of a good soccer player; by the age of ten, every player should be able to make the above moves.

When your team is evenly matched, your players will be on the attack only about 50 percent of the time. If your team is stronger and maintains ball possession about 60 to 70 percent of the time, your players are controlling the game. In high-level soccer, this control usually permits your team to win because you are also probably not making too many defensive errors. In youth soccer, even when your team is dominating the game with offensive play, it could easily lose if several defensive mistakes are made. This is something to think about. Defense is a paramount tactic. It is more important than offense, especially in outdoor soccer, where so few goals are scored. All players should learn defensive play because when they are without the ball, they will all be defenders, just as they are all on the attack when they have possession of it, including the goalkeeper. Defense is discussed in great detail in Chapter 4, but one piece of advanced information about defense is worth noting at this point. When a player is on defense and near an opponent who is dribbling the ball, he must not commit himself and go for the ball. The defensive player must maintain a position of staying goal side of the ball. This is called placing pressure on the opponent. It must be emphasized that the defending player need not try to tackle the ball from the opponent. There is a time to make a tackle and a time not to make a tackle. If the dribbling player makes a dribbling mistake, it is only then that there is a chance to dislodge the ball from the opponent safely. In time, players automatically know when this occurs. If it does not occur, then the defender is to retain a steady retreating pace with the opponent. This pressure forces the opponent either to attempt a pass or to make a dribbling mistake. This is quality defense, but an impulsive defensive move can cause a goal to be scored against your team and can also lose the game for you. The necessity for self-control in a defender cannot be over emphasized.

When not in possession of the ball, all of your players should be marking opponents. Of course the players cannot do this if they are not in top condition. Players must be taught at an early age to participate during the whole game, that is, to be constantly working. One thing to be on the alert for, however, is the performance of the so-called "star" players. They can sometimes be difficult to handle. Often they offer little in the way of defense after losing the ball to the opponents. They are often attackers but not defenders or team players. It should be noted that when goals are scored, it is important to give the whole team credit, for in reality the whole team scored the goal. And it is my opinion that it is immodest for the person who scored the goal to make some sort of a victory dance. In competitive soccer, teams are victorious because they play together and because the majority of the players on such a team are excellent.

Exceptional players are not too common. When you have one on your team, he may serve the team in a role that is more than just that of another player. It may be advisable to move this player into the center half back position in formations employing such a position. One reason for this is that even exceptional players do not score very often to save the day when playing against tough teams, but the whole team can become stronger because of on-the-field leadership. Players may just constantly perform better when a strong player is in the center half back position.

As a coach, show leadership by spending some time with the center half back and give her an explanation of the importance of winning loose balls, settling and shielding high and low balls, and making controllable passes to open teammates. These passes feed open teammates for constructive offensive buildups. Let that player know that you know the great asset she is to the team and that consistency and dependability are very important player assets. It should be pointed out that it is not too difficult for opponents to focus on a single star player, but it is very difficult for them to overcome a team that plays together.

League Control

If a soccer league has an overall plan to develop its youth to the fullest potential in this sport, it will have an overall plan for skill levels according to age groups. This is similar to the expectations set by our educational systems. Coaches should have freedom to instruct in their own particular style, but they should all be following certain guidelines for an achievement level according to the age group that they are instructing. Youth soccer is well past its infancy in North America. In some places, it is quite advanced, but in other places, soccer is growing in enrollment but very slowly in quality. Parents and coaches should insist on quality playing while getting away from brute force methods common in many clubs.

Allowing coaches total freedom to chose any style and method of instruction assumes that your child will automatically receive correct coaching. This can no more be true in soccer than it is in any instructional institution that does not have a curriculum. There should be guidelines. Without training guidelines, some coaches will completely contradict the teachings of other coaches, and who is right? In general, a pragmatic coaches' committee will be more often right than individual coaches. If such a committee is formed and is objective, eventually it could develop excellent guidelines that promote better soccer. It must be remembered that some coaches have little soccer or coaching experience. Some have experience from places where rough and tumble soccer is the norm. Some have experience where outdated long-ball soccer is the norm. It might be thought that all of this diversity of experience can blend into what is best for everyone, but I have never found this to be true. In general, there is such a mix of styles that exposure to many of them in the learning years often confuses young players. The better players in my opinion have nearly always been those who have one type of soccer background. Usually it has been with ethnic groups that play short-ball soccer, but occasionally I have seen it with players who have come from backgrounds where only long-ball soccer is the style of play.

From the standpoint of good team play soccer, modern short-ball soccer, the following negative practices should be avoided as much as possible to keep from giving your opponents the advantage. Disregarding any of these 21 points will give your opponents an advantage.

1. Indiscriminate kicking or heading the ball up field by any of the eleven players. There is possibly one exception to this rule. That is when the opponent's defense is up at the halfline and your team has fast and strong forwards. Care must be exercised here to avoid making this the rule and not the exception because this situation is not likely to occur against well matched teams.

2. Trying to trap a ball that is not within the reach of the trapping player (a sloppy trap), with the exception of the body trap, discussed in Chapter 3.

3. Throw-ins that are "up the line." These are discussed in detail in Chapter 3.

4. Flicking the ball with either the head or foot up-field.

5. Dribbling the ball more than 2' (.6 meter) ahead of the dribbling foot.

6. Air passes or throw-ins that cannot be controlled by the receiver.

7. Passes in front of your own goal.

8. Stabbing (tackling) at the ball while the carrier has control of it.

9. Dribbling the ball down the center of the field for long distances by a single player, especially after a kickoff.

10. Players having a difference of opinion with the referee.

11. Not passing to a near, open, unmarked teammate when that player has a better attack advantage, even if that player is behind the one with the ball.

12. Passing the ball in the manner called "threading the eye of the needle" in your own defense or midfield.

13. Scissor kicks.

14. Taking a shot on goal obstructed by an opponent while a near, unmarked teammate is in a nonoffside position.

15. Taking a near-zero angle shot on goal.

16. Attempting single-kick scoring on corner kicks (shooting directly into the goal from a corner kick).

17. Jumping in the air while attempting to dislodge a ball from a dribbling opponent.

18. Dribbling through two or more opponents simultaneously.

19. Tackling an opponent from behind.

20. Taking the ball away from one's own teammate.

21. Taking single-touch kicks ("once-on" kicks) more than 25' (7 ½ meters) in front of the goal; the distance becomes less then 25' when the angle to the goal decreases.

Parents' Participation

As a parent, you have a right to expect the soccer organization to have at least a general plan for the development of its soccer players. Obviously, a strict plan for their development is better, but one will usually hear that "we are doing the best we can do with the limited help available." A league charter for the progress of the player's development is very useful, however, as an instrument for improving skillful play. A charter gives a purpose to a league, whereas just seasonal soccer may serve only for recreation. This charter may state that the league's intention is to promote and develop skilled players through ball control and player self-control.

If you are interested enough in your child's development in this sport, you will have to volunteer, and if you have little or no experience in soccer, the job of age group coordinator could be an excellent place to start. Having this job means that you periodically inspect the practice of each team in your age group for conformance to the league's training requirements. Appropriate training, as deemed necessary by the league, will not occur without inspections and enforcement from its top level. Furthermore, training principles will need to be debated with those who are in the soccer game just to win games at any cost. But with a charter in place, the soccer will eventually be played on a more skillful level if the document is enforced. Whether or not you have the soccer background necessary for the job, you can be useful and effective; this book has been designed to help even the novice understand soccer. And if you are committed and no one is listening to you, other leagues will take in your child if you volunteer your services.

It is worthwhile to point out that as a parent, you have the responsibility for your own soccer player's development. Reminding the child to do homework drills and watch professional games on TV will help instill skills, inculcate respect for this sport, and help the child remain in the sport longer. The next section is broken down into two-year age groups to consider the children's potential development.

It is to be noted that uninterested parents of younger children sometimes think that the league provides some sort of baby sitting service. Be considerate to the coach and do not make it a practice for him to deliver or pick up your child.

With a few exceptions, soccer people are volunteers. Over the years, you may be a volunteer in just about any capacity, and it is in your child's own best interest to get quality training. You will foster this aim if you use your influence to promote ball control. If you are interested in developing your child's progress and self-confidence, as I have been in my own children's progress as well as longevity in the sport, you will need to comprehend that winning today's game is not a substitute for quality training.

Expected or Average Skill Levels by Age

The following are suggested "bench marks." At each "bench mark," your child should be able to perform all the skills discussed in that section prior to moving up to the next age group.

UNDER 10

This age group should be taught and encouraged to stay in their own zonal area most of the time. By the age of nine, they should not be following the ball around in the "beehive formation." Many stronger players in the younger age group assume that they can cover two or more zonal areas because their teammates are not effective in these areas. This must be discouraged because that only means that this same player will not be doing her own job effectively since one cannot be in two places at once. This does not mean that players cannot overlap into other zones. This is permissible as long as they have the speed and stamina to recover into their own position as required.

Trapping the ball dead (using the inside-of-the-foot trap) should be emphasized and expected at this level. Along with this, shielding should start to show up as a conscious effort. Passing the ball on the ground directly to teammates should occur often. One useful soccer skill is the ability to pass a ball in front of a running teammate to match his forward speed (forward not necessarily meaning towards the opponent's goal). This skill should be seen at least now and then.

At this age the players should know right from wrong in defense. It is right to back up with an opponent and wrong to "attack the ball" while it is under control of the dribbler. The coach and possibly others who understand this most valuable soccer principle should gently caution well-meaning spectators not to shout "get the ball." Players should be able to head moderate-speed balls and make good throw-ins about 70 percent of the time. On defense, they should know that they are to cover (get behind) each opponent on a throw-in and not let any opponent near the ball go unmarked. At this age level, field players should have a good comprehension of the basic skills discussed in Chapter 3 and be able to "win the loose ball."

The goalkeeper's training should encompass all of the skills of Chapter 6. The material in this chapter should be gradually covered during the entire season. The goalkeepers should have a separate trainer who works with them while the field players are performing the kicking, heading, trapping, shielding, and other drills. The goalkeepers are to adhere to their basic techniques until the more "advanced" catching and diving techniques start to come naturally. The goalkeepers' basics are punching and pushing out more balls than they are catching. Kicking balls up-field more often than throwing passes is the usual attack mode of novice goalkeepers, but they should be constantly reminded to start quick attacks with a throw instead of a kick. They should be taught that they are in charge of the defense: it is their responsibility not only to make saves, but to prevent having to make them as much as possible by recognizing and endeavoring to prevent defensive mistakes by their defensive players. They should be taught to direct each defensive winger to watch the opponent in each defensive zone and also remind them not to watch the ball. Do not expect much compliance in this area, but they should know by now to yell "goalkeeper" or "keeper" when they want the ball.

Goalkeepers will most likely take goals scored against them personally. Some goalkeepers cry or even have temper tantrums. They should be assured that there are always 10 other supporting players who let the goal against them occur.

UNDER 12

This age group should now be playing soccer in a fashion that sometimes resembles higher-level soccer. On-the-ground passes should be observed fairly frequently, and passes to teammates behind them (players nearer to their own goal) should be observed now and then. Defensive playing by all players should be observed occasionally without the necessity of coaches having to shout "apply pressure." Shielding and trapping should be attempted 50 percent of the time, and head passes to a teammate's feet (with difficult-to-control balls) should be observed a few times in each game. Defensive players should know by now that they must back up with an opponent dribbling the ball and also know that they are performing their jobs just as well by not ending up with the ball. They should be watching the opponent in their sector, not the ball, 75 percent of the time without first being reprimanded by the goalkeeper or coach. In this age group and lower, it is hoped that referees can be patient with coaches shouting commands to players. Coaches do need to shout explicit commands such as "get back," "kick it out" (kicking the ball over the sidelines in potentially goal-scoring situations for the opponents), "look for an open player," "watch the winger, not the ball," or "goalkeeper, call for the ball next time."

By this time children should have basic skills firmly implanted in their minds and bodies. If they are not up to this level, passing on advanced skills will not improve the missing basic skills and more time should be spent training them in the areas where they are lacking. If they are ready for new skills, these skills should be the following: Passing the ball back to the goalkeeper and other players who are more open than more forward players (naturally they must exercise good judgment near their own goal). Midfielders should be taught that it is their job to follow the forwards down-field to support the attacks. The defenders should also be able to move up-field to final distances where they can safely recover during counterattacks. In addition, the following particular skills in Chapter 7 should be introduced into this age group:

1. More about the instep kick
2. The duckbill instep kick
3. The front-volley and half-volley kicks
4. More about basic trapping
5. Under-the-foot trapping
6. Slide tackling
7. Shoulder charging

The goalkeeper should by now be rapidly passing off balls to the defending wings or midfielders 20 percent to 40 percent of the time. She should be tipping over or pushing out 50 percent to 60 percent of the balls shot on goal. Reminding the goalkeeper to call for the ball should now only occur rather infrequently during games. The goalkeepers should by now be somewhat aware that they need defensive players as part of their defensive strategy. They should be cognizant now that when they are alone between the ball and the goal, this third line of defense is the least desired defensive position to be in because a shot on goal has a decent chance of going between the goalposts. Protecting themselves (and the goal) with defending players in position should be seen about 50 percent of the time, that is, responsibility for the defense protecting the goal area should become a more common occurrence (this is the goalkeeper's second line of defense). At this time, goals that are scored against your team should be mentally recorded (or notes taken) to recapitulate the scene for discussion during the next training session to discuss defensive errors.

UNDER 14

This age group should be playing a controlled on-the-ground passing game even while under pressure for a good part of the game. Defensively, they should be able to stay with the opponent in their zone to neutralize many attacks. The midfield players should endeavor to control the game by settling loose balls and passing them off to players in open positions. These same players should be marking opponents during most of the game when their team is not in possession of the ball. Trapping of balls coming from long flights should be achieved quite often. The defensive players should be starting ground attacks quite often by trapping and settling the ball or by receiving passes from the goalkeeper. Shielding, slide tackling, backing up with attacking opponents, marking opposition players on their throw-ins, and good short passing should be seen quite often. Frontal volley kicks-on-goal should be seen only at close range. These kicks should now be controlled kicks and be on the mark or close to it. The following new skills should be introduced at this age level providing that the skills discussed in the previous section have taken hold:

1. The outside-of-the-foot kick
2. The under-the-body-instep kick
3. The side-volley kick
4. The blind-cross kick
5. Head trapping
6. The outside-of-the-foot trap
7. The dropping-ball trap
8. Shoulder charging (repeated)

The goalkeeper should now be making more catches, but still deflecting many balls, both over and to the sides of the goal. He should not be taking goals scored against his team too much to heart now. Taking over the defense should become slightly apparent by now, but for the most part, the goalkeeper will still be the last person on defense, making many saves at the expense of keeping defensive people in position. "Goalkeeper" should be audibly heard whenever the goalkeeper wants the ball. Approximately 40 percent of all the goalkeeper's attacks should be launched using your defense to carry the ball up-field, rather than "starting an attack" by kicking the ball up-field.

UNDER 16

At this level, their soccer is basically formed. If players come from teams or leagues where "kickball" was the style of play, they will have great difficulty unlearning that undisciplined type of play. It is impossible to learn ball control at this time, but it will probably be difficult to grasp under the pressure of game situations. It is about this time in undisciplined yet "talented" players' careers that they start to lose interest in the sport. They may not understand why, but it is mainly because they have lost their competitive edge in this sport. These players may be playing another sport and may not have developed that "edge" needed to be exceptional in one sport, let alone two sports.

On the other hand, skillful players at this age level have been fed a diet of proper soccer disciplines. This is often the case with the foreign-born players. These players probably inherited ball control techniques from several generations of skillful playing. The players in this age group should be playing with excellent ball control skills while under pressure, know what to do when they do not have the ball, know how to defend when the opponents possess the ball, and generally make everything that they do look easy. They have the ability to trap any ball and shield it, dribble through and around one player at a time, and back up defensively with an opponent dribbling the ball. They may even end up with the ball as a less skillful opponent tries to dribble past them. They know when and to whom to pass, they call out to nearby players low voice commands such as "man on," or "person on," "settle the ball, you're all alone," "carry the ball up-field," "pass it back," "left winger is open," "shoot," "move up the wing," "watch your opponent in your area," or anything else that is constructive. They are concentrating on the game all of the time, watching every player and everything that is going on in the game. While they still make mistakes, they make correct moves most of the time. Most importantly, when they are playing against a team that is stronger than their team, they do not revert to kickball. They maintain self-discipline to win loose balls, shield the ball to maintain its possession, and pressure the opponents. The smarter players with endurance often pressure the opposition to make mistakes. These players are consistent, while "star players" with "style" look good in average games but are usually unproductive in tough games. This is something to look for in tough games.

There are several new skills to be taught at this level:

1. The back-heel kick
2. The instep-stride kick
3. The toe poke
4. The thigh and calf traps
5. The standing tackle

The goalkeeper should be able to make diving saves, tip-overs, and tip-outs to the side of the goal as discussed in Chapter 5. Non-caught saves should never be pushed out to the center of the field at this level but should always be directed in an oblique angle to a part of the field that is considered safe territory. Most attacks started by the goalkeeper should start off with a thrown pass or a push-pass to a defender or midfielder in such a way that they can control the ball. Attacks that safely carry the ball beyond one's own midfield are actually the goalkeeper's first line of defense. By assuring that her own players will be in possession at the midfield, she is assuring that a counterattack is not immediately going to take place through an interception of the ball. If the teammates are not able to receive and shield the ball safely, however, the goalkeeper is forced to kick the ball upfield and take her chances that it will not be intercepted. By now the goalkeeper should command the defense-line players and have the confidence and authority to have any ball that she wishes. The goalkeeper knows by now which balls may be safely caught, safely pushed over or to the side, or punched out.

UNDER 19

The style of playing for the field players should be the same as that sometimes experienced with good younger players, but at this level such quality should be evident nearly all of the time. Goalkeepers should have developed total defensive control with all defensive players all of the time. The attacks should be launched using defensive players 80 to 90 percent of the time, that is, kicking the ball down to the forwards should occur very infrequently. Long diving, catching saves should be mastered fully, but this technique will not be needed too often if the first and second lines of defense are in place. Spectacular saves are often the cause of defensive errors that result when the goalkeeper is not in charge of the total defense.

The above paragraphs suggest a level of play that can be met by players if they have the desire to improve along with responsible guidance from adults in and around the soccer field. Ball control cannot be stressed enough. Some countries send teams to compete for the world cup that do not have ball control based upon proper shielding. Teams without ball control have difficulty making the playoffs.

Habits of Players with Style Not Skill

Professionals usually have the knowledge and ability to remain cool under pressure. Those who let their emotions rule them are usually inhibited from playing well. Professionals must spend countless hours training themselves in order to perform properly when under pressure. It is in their own best interests to remain calm even when others may not be calm. There are also those who do not develop the skills needed for top performance, but they may develop style. Style often replaces high skill levels and can be entertaining. It may even be useful in medium- to low-level competition. It does not, however, produce desired results in high-level competition.

By following players through the years, I was able to track the consistent and dependable players as well as the undependable players (players with enough style to fool some coaches). Unfortunately for everyone, these players with style remain in games longer then the consistent workhorses, who may only have a few real skills. The players with style may make some serious soccer mistakes, but they are allowed to remain in the game, whereas these workhorses may make about two mistakes and are often substituted out of the game. For the prudent coach's information, it may be worthwhile to point out some of the things these players with style tend to do:

1. Make long runs from their defensive area to the opposing defensive area, losing the ball.

2. Juggle the ball off the field of play. This is a more stylish than useful soccer technique.

3. Make bicycle kicks.

Note that both techniques 2 and 3 have been performed successfully by some famous soccer players, but for the most part these techniques do not help win games.

4. Participate fully in an attack on goal as a defense person, but get caught up-field when needed in their own defensive areas.

5. Constantly make long headers up-field, when a head or chest trap or a short head pass should give their team ball possession.

6. Sometimes gets away with a 180-degree blind turn near an opposing player (not making shielded turns).

7. Participates only during an attack and does not participate in applying defensive pressure.

8. Looks sharp in practice or easy games but is non-constructive in pressure-type, highly competitive games.

9. Takes an almost zero angle shot on goal, even when there is a non-offside, unmarked close teammate in an advantageous position.

10. Constantly makes air passes because of an inability to control the ball under pressure.

11. Constantly thinks that yardage is important and also always makes throw-ins "up the line."

12. As goalkeeper constantly makes remarkable saves to cover up for her inability to control the defense.

13. Makes unnecessary long kicks that amount to a counterattack against you. (Track this scene carefully as it may take six to eight touches on the ball before a counterattack results from this unnecessary kick.)

The list can be much longer, but these examples should illustrate the point that players who follow the teachings of good coaches should be noticed and given more game time than selfish players. As a point of observation, these selfish players frequently end their soccer career between the ages of 15 and 17. Players that accept valid coaching practices have the potential to become good or great athletes.

In summary, pressure often causes the amateur field player to lose his self-control and the perspective of the environment around him. This can be observed with players who do excessive running about, do not trap the ball in pressure situations, and make difficult-to-control passes to teammates. It is also observed in goalkeepers who throw their gloves on the ground or sulk after a goal is scored. The professional is consistent and dependable, while the amateur is hot one day, cold another day, and cannot be counted upon to perform in tough games. The professional controls himself, performs as trained, and is cognizant of his environment at all times. This player remains cool and gives soft verbal commands to teammates; he has aggressive determination and a consistently high spirit. This player has the skills and uses them under pressure, does not seek credit for his leadership, takes the sport seriously, improves his weaknesses on his own, and most importantly, never quits; this person is a professional. Naturally, entry-level players are not near a professional level nor should you expect them to be during their first years in soccer. If there is no leadership objective, however, you may never see great players coming out of your league.

3. Basic Skills
for Field Players

Basic skills, as has been already stressed, are the most important aspect of soccer playing, but they are deemphasized in training far too often for the seemingly more important need for game strategy. A player will not go far in this game without these skills, however. This chapter is devoted to basic skills, and they will be discussed in a more or less chronological learning order of importance.

Dribbling

Dribbling a soccer ball is what all eleven soccer players do. Even goalkeepers dribble at times. It should not be discouraged. It is the coach's responsibility to build players' confidence for dribbling the ball under the pressure of game situations. Often coaches try to discourage dribbling in games because they are apprehensive that the player will lose the ball to the opposition team. Yet they allow players to make long kicks or head balls down-field where there is usually about a 70 percent probability that the other team will end up with the ball anyway. There is more of a chance of losing the ball by making a long and indiscriminate up-field kick or a long header than by properly dribbling the ball and shielding it. Modern soccer, unlike some other sports, is not a game of possessing yardage, but one of ball possession and continuity through continuous clear passing. Often there is no near unmarked player, so the player with the ball should maintain possession until an unmarked teammate becomes available.

Of course, a distinction should be made between a team player who dribbles the ball looking for opportunities for the team and a player who is a "ball hog."

Young players must be taught the correct way to dribble because invariably they do it incorrectly. They dribble the ball by tapping it with their feet, and the end result is that it moves beyond their near reach and out of their control. They do not protect it. They also watch the ball while dribbling it. All of this must be corrected.

Point number one for ball dribbling is not to tap the ball, but to push it. Tapping causes sharp, uncontrollable impulses, while pushing it causes controlled follow-through movements. The pushing or dribbling is done by using the outside or inside of the foot at any time, in any order as needed. With the inside of the foot dribble, the ball is generally contacted well in front of the ankle or it may be under it to protect it better.

Constantly using the outside-of-the-foot dribble (against the top of the three smaller toes) is effective when dribbling up to a single opponent whom one wishes to fake and pass. For example, when you wish to pass an opponent on the right, come directly towards that player, pushing the ball with only the outside of the right foot while slowing down your speed to enable you to touch the ball every time your right foot gets out in front. At about 4' (1.2 meters) in front of the opponent, feint to the left and push the ball with the same point of contact of the right foot again, but this time at a 45-degree angle to your right (the opponent's left). The fake is now completed, and you should be past the defender. This maneuver is further discussed in Chapter 4 — "Fakes."

Inside-of-the-foot dribbling can also be effective when a player, who needs absolute control of the ball, is coming up to an opponent. If the opponent tries to tackle the ball, it is easily maneuvered out of her way, and the dribbler can then pass this opponent. Another choice is to push the ball through the opponent's legs (if they are open). The inside-of-the-foot dribble is accomplished in the following way: while approaching the opponent, each foot that is in front must touch the ball with every step to maintain control over it. The dribbling player should be looking around the field and not down at the ball.

When one is just maneuvering the ball, either foot and contact point may be interchanged at any moment in time. The important

Photo 1. The technique of dribbling the ball near the feet must be learned for ball control. Notice the outstretched arms that give the player the balance necessary to change direction immediately if it becomes necessary.

rule to remember is to keep the ball as close to the feet as possible. Note that: only when a player is dribbling in open spaces can the ball be dribbled at a slightly further distance from the feet. Photo 1 shows a player dribbling the ball close to his feet even though there is no opponent immediately in front of him.

Players should be taught that they must dribble with their head up in order to be in control of the ball and have awareness of the opponents' positions. This comes with practice. There are times, however, when a player must be looking at the ball: these times occur when the player is in close contact with an opponent (shielding the ball) and just before and during kicking, trapping, and heading. The drills both at practice and at home will teach players to dribble with their heads up and their eyes searching for opportunities and advancing opposing players.

As mentioned above, it is important to slow down when dribbling towards an opponent because ball control should not be sacrificed for speed. This is especially important when approaching the opponents' goal while coming face to face with defenders. Very often players will try to dribble between two defenders to get a shot on goal. This type of try is seldom successful, and it should not be encouraged. In a situation where a player is coming upon two or three defenders, the best option is usually to stop and pass the ball back to an attack-supporting teammate. Dribbling is further discussed in the sections on shielding.

Basic Trapping

All players can kick the ball to some degree. They can do this instinctively even though their kicking needs to be perfected. Correct trapping techniques must be learned early in one's soccer career; therefore the basic trapping techniques are discussed first. We will start by considering the trapping that is used most of the time in a ball control soccer game. The trap is made with the inside of the foot just below the ankle (see Fig. 3-1-A and 3-1-B). Note the point of contact on the foot. The ball should go down after one traps it. If the trapping foot is too high, the ball will roll under it, and if it is too low, the ball will bounce up high. A safe assumption, when one is trapping a ball, is that there will be an opponent very close by. This means that the player must go to the ball rather then wait for it to come to him.

This trap, as all traps, follows certain rules and sequences:

RULE 1. **Keep your eye on the ball.** This is important when kicking, trapping, and heading.

RULE 2. **Go to the ball.** Never wait for it to come to you.

RULE 3. **Stop.** Just before you make contact with the ball, you should stop. It is extraordinarily difficult to trap a ball while you are in motion.

RULE 4. **Trap and shield.** As soon as the impact of the ball is felt, soften that impact by moving the foot away from the ball. The ball must stop dead. The ball must go down with the trap. If it goes up, too much time will be required to settle it. Immediately shield it.

RULE 5. **Move out.** This next move is to immediately push-off the ball in a direction free from the space of an opponent. This is very important because, as any experienced player knows, it is necessary to immediately accelerate with the ball in order to maintain its possession.

RULE 6. **Do not turn blindly.** With the ball under control, move only to your front, no matter which direction you are facing. Turning blindly with the ball is a sure way to lose it to an opponent. Turning is covered in these sections: "Turning While Shielding" and "Shielding on the Touch Line."

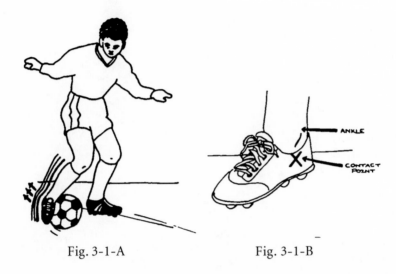

Fig. 3-1-A   Fig. 3-1-B

Figure 3-1. The inside-of-the-foot trap. Note the shock absorption movement of the trapping foot moving away from the ball and point of contact.

Heading

When heading the ball, it is necessary to keep one's eyes on the ball and open during contact. Basic heading practice should start with close throws from another player or coach or use the ball rebound board described in Chapter 6. Certain balls such as rubber or very hard leather ones are not recommended for heading drills because impact with them can be painful. A recommended drill is to have players waiting in line and standing about 8' (2½ meters) from the thrower. The ball is thrown underhanded, starting the throw with the ball at knee level. Each player gets three successive headers (more if the player cannot get it right). The repetitions are necessary for reinforcement of the skill. See Fig. 3-2 for the proper method of heading.

The power that is needed comes from using the back and neck to propel the ball. It is best to head the ball parallel to the ground or even downwards. If the player consistently causes the ball to rise, the player must learn to get her head slightly over the center of the ball. There are times in games when a player must head the ball far away with a

Figure 3-2. Heading. Note that the center of the forehead is the point of contact. Following through the header makes the ball's flight more accurate. Practice heading with the eyes open.

slightly elevated angle. There is not much need to practice this: when a player becomes skillful in the heading techniques, this variation will come naturally. During the drills, the players should be encouraged to head the ball horizontally or slightly downwards.

Shielding

Shielding or protecting the ball is the most basic skill that must be learned for ball control mastery. Modern soccer is a game of ball possession. This skill will enable any field player to maintain possession at all times against a single opponent and possibly against two opponents. But against three opponents, even the best ball handler will probably lose the ball. Shielding against one opponent is extremely effective, however. To exemplify this skill, players that are familiar with basketball should draw the comparison with a dribbling player. The basketball player instinctively places his back to an opponent when dribbling. Even though it is not instinctive in soccer, the technique is the same: the back is used to screen the ball. When a player becomes skillful at shielding, this player will have developed a base upon which to build many other soccer skills.

Control is the hallmark of professional play. Ball control is the ability to get the ball from point A to point B — to a teammate or into the goal. Ball control starts by shielding with the body while one is moving and looking around for the best opportunity. If a player does not shield the ball immediately upon receiving it (positioning the body between the ball and the opponent immediately with trapping) and while in possession of it, that player will never be any better than an average player. The best of professional players are expert at shielding and that helps make everything that they do look easy.

RECEIVING THE BALL

When two players from opposing teams are going for the loose ball or a pass, the one who gets to it first will end up with it if she starts to trap the ball and immediately places her body between the opponent and the ball. Then it is important to arch the back towards the opponent without contacting her. This will further separate the opponent from the ball. See Fig. 3.3. (Note that this is not obstruction. Obstruction would be endeavoring to gain possession of the ball by blocking the opponent's path to the ball, that is, running between the opponent and the ball.) At this moment, the ball is isolated and must be pushed into open space away from the opponent; it must always be kept out of reach of the opponent's feet. The opponent should be kept in view at all times with one's peripheral vision or by watching the opponent's shadow. One should never place the ball between oneself and the opponent and should never step on the ball to change direction while shielding. Stepping on the ball is reserved for other tactics, not for ball control or shielding.

DRIBBLING

When one is dribbling near an opponent, the ball must always be kept on the opposite side from this person. This also means that when a dribbling player is approached by an opponent, he immediately gets his body between the ball and the other player. If this same dribbling player is having difficulty advancing in a forward direction, then an alternate direction must be chosen. It may mean making a U-turn and heading back towards his own goal. Awkward as it may sound, it is effectively simple and perfectly acceptable to pass the ball back to the

Figure 3-3. Shielding immediately upon receiving the ball. This is accomplished by placing one's body between the ball and the opponent while settling it. The arms must be lowered after gaining balance.

goalkeeper or a defender. Players must get the thought out of their heads that forward movement for players and the ball is the only acceptable practice. With the "Monkey in the Middle" drill in Chapter 6, the players may move in any direction when they possess the ball. This drill replicates ball control and possession exactly as in a game situation and is highly instructive for this purpose: the player receives the ball, shields and dribbles it clearly away from an "opposition" player, and then passes it to the "teammate" not marked by this same "opposition" player.

While in possession of the ball (as illustrated in Fig. 3-3), the player should be instructed that he has every right to protect it. As this player improves in this area, so will his self-confidence, so encourage dribbling with shielding. The first choice should be to run with the ball (dribbling) towards open spaces to search for a player who is in a favorable position for a clear pass, to set up a play or to score. The run could be to dribble diagonally across the field and then up-field on the opposite wing. The run could be long or short. It could be from one of the up-field wings, bringing the ball back to deliver it to the goal-keeper, who in turn may pass it off to an open winger on the opposite side of the field. The run could be forward, backward, diagonal or zigzag, but it must be purposeful. The players should be reminded not to go to the right, then to the left, and back to the right again or vice versa. Staying in a local area will draw opponents quickly. If a play-maker player such as the center half back settles and shields the ball, the best play might be to shoot over a ground pass in front of an open high speeding teammate. It is advantageous for one teammate to set-tle, control, and shield a ball that is difficult to deal with and then pass it on the ground in front of an open teammate who is running at top speed up-field. This unselfish play gains a time advantage and often takes the opposition by surprise; moreover, it may produce an effective attack on the opponent's goal. Note that it useful to instruct players always to be thinking ahead and planning moves to be used if and when the ball comes to them.

It is necessary to point out that some aggressive players will hack at the legs of a shielding player. The dribbler should not become intim-idated by such a tactic but should maintain her body between the aggressive opponent and the ball and not allow this player to get the best of her. One must always remember to keep the ball at a safe dis-tance while shielding. The referee should not penalize the dribbler for any contact between the two players as long as the dribbler does not foul the opponent. On the other hand, the referee should be aware of the hacking and warn players of serious fouls letting them know the offense has not gone unnoticed. Note that the referee is within his rights to allow infractions created by the opponent to go unpunished and allow the playing to continue because of the advantage rule. That rule is not to stop the play and give the advantage to the perpetrator of an offense when a member of the other team is in possession of the ball.

Shielding and dribbling go together to maintain ball possession. The shielding technique is perfected as one's dribbling gets better. Dribbling well and with skill is achieved through practice. The type of dribbling is simple. It is performed using only the inside of the foot or the outside of the foot, and the ball must never be placed between the dribbler and the opponent. (See Figs. 3-4-A and 3-4-B.) This technique is simple once the method is understood. Players who shield well and then lose the ball usually make the last "fatal" mistake. They keep the ball from the opponent by applying the appropriate shield-ing with an arched back towards the opponent and using the inside and

Fig. 3-4-A. Outside of the foot   Figure 3-4-B. Inside of the foot

Figure 3-4. Moving with a shielded ball. Note that the ball is simply pushed with either the inside or outside of either foot. There are only four moves — using the inside of either foot and the outside of either foot to keep the ball out of reach of the opponent.

outside of the foot to maneuver the ball but they lose the ball either by stepping on it or by putting it between the opponent and themselves. Stepping on the ball as a feint places the ball near the opponent where it cannot be properly shielded. Note that stepping on the ball can be an effective move when dribbling at high speed down the wing with an opponent close behind. When the ball is stepped on at this time, it places the opponent in a non-strategic position: the dribbler surprisingly brakes himself, and the momentum of player in pursuit carries him well past the ball. But since this technique is outside the realm of ball control, it is best to avoid it, at least with inexperienced players.

TURNING

As mentioned earlier, turning blindly is not a smart move. Sometimes players get away with turning blindly, but it is not in the player's or team's best interests to make this a practice because it is not necessary when a player has mastered the shielding turn. The turn can be made as follows: if a dribbling player is facing her own goal, naturally the desire is to turn 180 degrees. The player should always rotate in the direction towards the closest touch line if there is room for a turn.

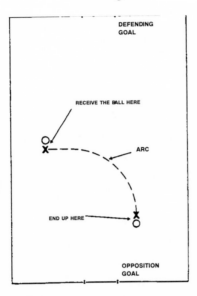

Figure 3-5. Turning with the ball.

Rotating towards the farthest touch line places the ball in or near the center of her own goal area as the turn takes place: The turn will take place in a circular motion and put the player closer to the center of the goal than she was located prior to the start of the turn. This move can place the ball too close to her own goal.

With the opponent always in view, the player should rotate in a more or less quarter-circle by constantly pushing the ball with the outside of the foot in a hooked manner. For instance, if the player is facing her own goal and has a touch line nearer to her right (with, say, 8' [2.4 meter] to spare), the player will push the ball with the outside of the right foot while continuously revolving in a clockwise rotation as in Fig. 3-4-A. If the player is not near her own goal, either direction of rotation is all right, as illustrated in Fig. 3-5. Note that the ball is constantly shielded as shown in Fig. 3-6 and also that the dribbler is illustrated balancing herself, not pushing-off the opponent. The opponent is kept at a distance from the ball by an arched back as shown in Fig. 3-7. There will inevitably be some light contact here, but since the player without the ball will be doing the crowding, any foul that is called by the referee should not be against the dribbler.

Figure 3-6. Shielding while turning.

ON THE TOUCH LINE

When a player with the ball is being crowded against the touch line, execute the shielding moves facing the touch line while keeping the opponent at a distance with the shoulder that is leaning into him. It must be certain that the opponent is making contact with the dribbler and not vice versa. When keeping an opponent away, the dribbling is to be done with either foot, using the inside and the outside of the foot. If the opponent is blocking the right side as shown in Fig. 3-7, the dribbler's right shoulder is against his chest (if the opponent is making contact). The ball is being played with the left foot, so the player will have to move in towards the center of the field to get free to make the next move. If the opponent positions himself at the dribbler's opposite side, on the defending goal side, the dribbler should move up the field along the touch line. The rule is to always push the ball in the direction where your opponent is not situated.

A FINAL NOTE ON SHIELDING

It may seem to the reader that I am placing an exaggerated or even dogmatic emphasis on shielding. There is a reason for this. If shielding is overlooked and/or is considered just another soccer technique, the reader has not really grasped what modern control ball soccer is all about. Shielding is essential, but common sense must prevail.

Figure 3-7. Shielding against the touch line.

Shielding is the heart of ball control and is effective against one opponent. As mentioned earlier, it can even be somewhat effective against
two players, but against three players it is extremely difficult to maintain possession of the ball. If a player has drawn three opponents close
to himself, the best option would be to pass the ball off to a nearby
player: drawing three opponents should leave nearby teammates
unmarked. Trying to out dribble three opponents is a sure way of
turning the ball over to the other side. If the previously mentioned conditions do not exist, a player has control of the ball only if he can protect it while trapping it or dribbling it under pressure. Playing soccer
without this skill is playing the sport at about the lowest level.

It is important to instruct dribbling players about the following
situation. Some players have a tendency to get trapped in a corner, free
themselves, and get trapped once again. They should be instructed to
steer themselves and the ball in some general direction, being careful
not to remain in one spot for more then a few seconds. If necessary, a
forward player may find it necessary to dribble the ball back to her own
goal area and pass the ball off to the goalkeeper. The goalkeeper may
be the best player to pass the ball to, and the players should be
instructed to comply with this idea. If the team members are trained
in ball-handling skills from a young age, they will come to depend

Photo 2. Shielding in action. This photo clearly illustrates the value of shielding property.

upon the goalkeeper as another teammate on the field, not just the defender of the goal. The goalkeeper can usually change fields more safely than another player: the goalkeeper can receive a pass from the left side of the field, for example, and quickly roll the ball to the right side of the field. This maneuver keeps your team in possession of the ball and on the offense, but a long kick up-field may place your team on the defense.

One last reminder about shielding. Players should not become intimidated when an opponent is body pushing them as they shield the ball. They must be aware of this tactic and resist opponent body-shoving by stiffening their own body, while maintaining the ball as far from the opponent's feet as possible as they shield it. Shielding is an art and must be tried and practiced to master it correctly. When it is mastered, a shielding player in a one-against-one situation should never lose the ball. Photo 2 illustrates shielding in action. The player with the ball is actually heading in the direction of his own defending goal and has clearly maintained its possession.

Defending

This book stresses many more offensive techniques than defensive ones because there are relatively few defensive techniques in comparison to the offensive ones. These few defensive measures must, however, be ingrained into each player. Offensive mistakes in general are not too significant, but even one defensive mistake can cost you the game. Error-free games in regards to defense can win you games if your team scores one goal, and with no goals scored, they can keep you from losing games. So defensive awareness is a necessity for all players. Every player must learn to be a defender.

Whenever the other team has the ball, your whole team is on the defense and each player must be constantly reminded to mark person to person, except possibly in your own defensive area, where zone defense is probably the defensive tactic. The coach should realize that those players who do not need the constant reminding about applying defensive pressure are the team workers. These workers are actually helping the offense because their pressure will cause the other team to make mistakes, turning the ball over to your side more frequently.

Pressure on an opponent may be applied in various ways. When one of your players is "on the heels" of an opponent dribbling down the field towards your own goal, your player is naturally distracting the dribbler. This desirable pressure often is assisted by one of your team players who may be heading towards the dribbler at an oblique angle and often just sweeps the ball away from the dribbler. This defensive teamwork is actually a two-person tackle. Another and most important pressure comes, however, when one of your players positions himself in front of a dribbling opponent, backs up with the opponent, and constantly remains goal side of this dribbling player. While employing this tactic, the defending player must remain cool and rely upon his defensive training: skillful dribblers, however, often bait the defending player to go for the ball to tackle it. Rarely if ever, however, will the tackling player end up with the ball while it is under the control of a skilled dribbler. When a defending player instinctively goes for the ball, the most usual occurrence is that this defending player ends up with "egg on his face" as the dribbler passes by. The best defensive move for the defender is to keep a safe distance from the dribbler while backing up with this advancing player. Slowing the player down while screening a potential shot on goal allows the goalkeeper time to set herself into position for the shot, if it comes. See Fig. 3-8 for the correct defensive posture. As noted earlier, this defensive maneuver

Figure 3-8. Correct defensive posture. (1) Keep eyes on the ball. (2) Keep legs closed. (3) Stay on toes. (4) Keep balance with outstretched arms. (5) Do not commit oneself while letting the opponent come forward.

by a defense person is the goalkeeper's second line of defense. A mistake here breeches that line of defense, and the defense must then rely upon the goalkeeper to save any shots on goal (the team's last line of defense).

It has often been said to me that sooner or later the defender must commit himself. I do not believe this because my experience has always reinforced the above principle. I have seen professionals mistakenly go for the ball and miss it, resulting in a goal. This severe defensive error causes a re-positioning of defensive players. The confused goalkeeper is then immediately placed into an unpredictable situation while getting himself into an unbalanced position.

There is a correct defensive procedure consisting of the following: The correct distance must be maintained. This distance between the defender and the attacker depends on the attacker's potential speed and the defender's potential speed. If the defender is too close, the opponent can get by her. If the defender is too far, the attacker will have enough space for a clear pass or a clear shot on goal. In time each player will learn to make the necessary adjustments to perform this tactic correctly. The defender must back up and continue to do so until she is about 10' (3 meters) from the goal, and he must be constantly reminded to do so. With other defenders and the goalkeeper close by, there is little room into which the attacker can now steer herself. This procedure is about the only safe tactic that can constrain an attacker. If the attacker does not lose control of the ball, the defender does not attempt to dislodge the ball from the attacker. If the opponent takes a shot on goal and the defender is at a correct distance from the attacker (and has her legs closed), an experienced goalkeeper can usually predict the way the shot is going to be made and be in position to make the appropriate moves.

The above method of defense is sound and effective, but it is the most difficult tactic to instill into people, perhaps because it seems unnatural not to go for the ball when another individual is dribbling it. However unnatural it may seem, backing up with a player who has full control of a dribbled ball is effective, providing self-discipline is employed. It should be noted that it takes patience to wait for the opponent to lose the slightest control of the ball. It takes training to develop the timing, coordination, and balance. Note also that this effectiveness needs to be relearned after remaining out of practice for only a few months.

Body Traps

This is a very interesting and useful trap but is not a trap in the usual sense of trapping. The ball is not settled dead at one's feet, as is desired with other traps. It is employed when the ball is descending sharply from the air and begins to bounce seemingly uncontrollably. The "trap" is performed by settling the ball down and bringing it under control as follows: When possible, the player should align his body directly behind the directional path of the ball and run after it in pursuit. When in contact with it, guide it in some preferred direction with any part of the body (except the arm or hand) until it slows down. This could occur with the knee, stomach, head, etc.; push it in the direction of open space until it is under control by the feet. (See Fig. 3-9.) If an opponent tries to get to a bouncing ball first and your player is not able to align himself with the ball, he should position himself to push the ball off in a direction not obvious to the opponent and when near the ball apply shielding as though he had just received the ball. Then your player follows the ball until it is under total control with the feet while also being properly shielded.

Figure 3-9. The body trap. To get the best control of a bouncing ball, it is necessary to align oneself with the trajectory of the ball. This "trap" may be settled 30' to 40' from the ball's initial bodily contact.

Instep Kicks

It should be noted that while the theme of this book is to promote modern on-the-ground soccer, there are times when the ball will have to be kicked relatively long distances in the air. As players mature and learn to keep the ball on the ground as much as possible, the airborne balls will be less common, but will still be used now and then. The ball can be kept low if the nonkicking foot is placed in such a way that the toes of this foot are alongside the front of the ball as shown in Fig. 3-10-A. This kick is useful for scoring goals, but the shot must be kept low. Shooting for the lower corners is best for outdoor soccer, while shooting for the upper corners is best for indoor soccer. Shooting for the upper corner in indoor soccer requires only a slightly elevated kick, and players are reminded to keep the nonkicking foot forward to prevent shots from rising above the goal. This kick is useful for goal kicks; when changing fields (that is, when passing the ball from one side of the field to the other side), the ball may be kicked up into the air if the receiver has room to settle the ball. It is used for defensively clearing the ball and sometimes for passing.

The basic instep kick (for small feet) is shown in Fig. 3-10-B. It is performed by kicking the ball with the laced portion of the foot. The

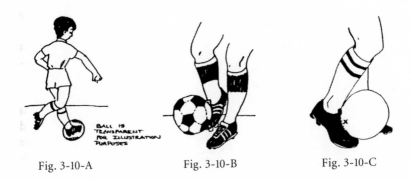

Fig. 3-10-A   Fig. 3-10-B   Fig. 3-10-C

Figure 3-10. The instep kick. Note the nonkicking foot position. The knee of the kicking leg is over the ball. Fig. 3-10-B illustrates the basic instep kick for small feet. Figure 3-10-C illustrates the angled instep kick: the foot must be turned out.

kick is kept low by placing the nonkicking foot near the ball with the toes approximately even with the front of the ball. This position places the body over the ball during the kick and is needed for accuracy as well as for keeping the kicked ball low.

The angled instep kick is for players with shoe sizes above size 8, who will have difficulty performing the basic instep kick without modifying it slightly. This modified version is illustrated in Fig. 3-10-C. In the modified version, the kicking foot must be turned slightly outward (getting the toes out of the way). If this is not accomplished, the foot will probably contact the ground before meeting the ball. The ball will now be met on the right side by a right-footed kick, causing it to spin counterclockwise, thus curving it to the left. The nonkicking foot is placed in front of the ball (as in the basic instep kick) to position the kicker's weight over the ball to keep the ball flight low. To elevate the ball for long goal kicks or to change fields, the nonkicking foot is not placed as far forward. The toes will be at about midline of the ball instead of at the ball's front.

Kicking a ball should be done with precision. When making any kick, the following Rules 1 to 4 will always apply. For the instep kick, Rule 5 is added. These rules are:

RULE 1. **Keep your eye on the ball.**
Look at the target, then look at the ball and keep your eye on it while

kicking and during the follow-through. The best practice is to keep the head down until the ball gets to the target.

Note that the practice of looking up immediately after the kick is made can give the kicker a tendency to look up prematurely, causing non-compliance with this most important rule.

RULE 2. **Follow through the kick.**

Kicks are governed by the laws of mechanics. Following through is necessary to give the ball accuracy and speed: the accuracy is attained because the ball will follow the path of the foot aimed at the target, and more speed can be attained by having the foot contact the ball for a longer accelerating period of time. The follow through allows the kicker to kick with less than her maximum power (for accuracy) but still have sufficient speed.

RULE 3. **Kick in a straight line.**

Do not kick in an arched fashion either from side to side or from down to up. For example, mentally note the mechanics of the flight of the ball when the kick is made by swinging the leg in an arc from right to left. This is equivalent to rotating a ball on a string from right to left. At the moment that the string is released, the ball will follow the tangent path line that it has at that instant. The kicked ball will follow the tangent path the moment that the foot and ball part contact. (It is difficult to pinpoint the exact moment of this release time.) In both examples, the precise flight directions are difficult to control accurately. Therefore a straight-line kick is the optimum kick.

RULE 4. **Compensate for the ball spin.**

The mechanics of a spinning ball cause it to curve. Whenever a moving ball spins, it creates a lowered air pressure (because of the spin) on the opposite side of the kick. It is going to curve towards that low pressure direction unless it is counteracted by the wind. In soccer, the curve ball (relative to the goal) is usually referred to as an in-swinger (sometimes called a banana kick). The reverse curvature is called an out-swinger. Fig. 3-11 illustrates these kicks. For long kicks, the player must learn to compensate for the spin. If the kick is made at the center of the ball, no left or right spin will occur.

RULE 5. **Place the nonkicking foot forward.**

When it is desired to keep the instep kick low, always place the non-kicking foot with the toes at the front position of the ball.

Push Passes

One of the best ways to send an accurate pass to a nearby player is by using the push pass. This is not exactly a kick; as the name implies,

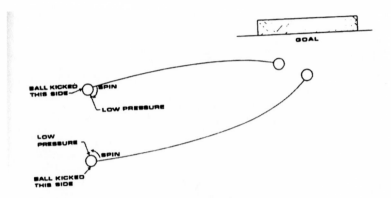

Figure 3-11. The in-swinger vs. the out-swinger kick.

it is actually a push pass. The ball is pushed with the inside of the foot at the same point of contact as is used in the inside-of-the-foot trap. (See Fig. 3-1-B.) Some people initially find this push pass difficult to learn, but they find it easy once they realize that both legs must squat prior to its execution. (See Fig. 3-12.) This technique is also excellent for shooting on goal while dribbling or for running up to a ground-ball cross (a ball passed in front of the goal) for a close once-on shot. With the large surface area of the instep behind the ball, it is easy to compensate for slight errors in the exact point of contact. It is more reliable to use this kick on a ground-crossed moving ball (within 25' [7½ meters] of the goal) than for kicking the crossed ball with the front part of the foot.

The Chest Traps

The chest is very effective for controlling either a high ball coming from the air or one that is bouncing at the player from the ground. It is important to follow these rules to keep the ball from either bouncing far from the chest or deflecting too far to either side of the player attempting to make the trap. (See Fig. 3-13-A.)

RULE 1. **Keep your eye on the ball** during the entire trap.
RULE 2. **Go to the ball** and align yourself with the trajectory of the ball. Alignment is very important because any angle to the trajectory will

Figure 3-12. The inside-of-the-foot pass (push pass). Note that the nonkicking foot and the knee are pointed to the target. The kicking foot and knee are at a right angle to the target. The nonkicking leg is bent from the knee about 20 degrees.

cause the ball to deflect to the right or left of the body and be difficult to bring under control. The ball should impact the center of the chest just above the sternum. (The sternum is where one feels bone intersect with the soft stomach tissue.)

RULE 3. **Stop** just before the time of impact.

RULE 4. *__Position the chest__ to be approximately perpendicular to the flight of the ball.

RULE 5. **At the moment of impact, withdraw the chest** to soften the impact. The ball should go down or level, not up, when this trap is performed correctly, but when chest trapping a ball coming from steeply inclined trajectories, the ball will rise.

RULE 6. **Immediately dribble and shield the ball** in any direction other than the direction from which the opponent is coming.

*Females are permitted to trap the ball with the contact made to the forearms as shown in Fig. 3-13-B.

Throw-Ins

Throw-ins are given to the team that did not touch the ball last when it went over the touch line. Throw-ins are so simple that it is hard

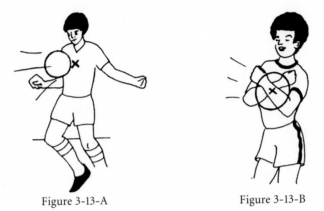

Figure 3-13-A   Figure 3-13-B

Figure 3-13. Chest trapping. Fig. 3-13-A illustrates the ball coming at the player from either a low or a high position. Fig. 3-13-B shows how a female can protect herself while chest trapping.

to make them incorrectly, but players make mistakes because they insist upon doing it their own way by taking a running start. When done incorrectly, the throw is awarded to the other side. Therefore in high-level soccer, it is most common to see good throw-ins made by players who remain stationary while having both legs in the same frontal position, that is, neither foot ahead of the other. See Fig. 3-14 for the positioning of the body, feet, and ball.

The following steps will allow a player to make consistently good throw-ins: The back is arched backwards, and the ball is behind the head. One or both feet can be standing on the touch line. If the thrower decides to throw the ball in a different direction than he originally intended, he should realign himself to face the target before making the throw. The ball must be released only after passing it over the face. It is difficult to perform a throw very slowly to a close player. Some inexperienced referees may call it a bad throw-in, however, even though it has been executed correctly. Because it is a little difficult to throw a very slow throw-in correctly, it is usually not done.

The following bad practices cause a referee to award the throw-in to the other team and generally occur when the thrower takes a running start.

Figure 3-14. Throw-ins. Note that the feet are in the same frontal position, the ball is behind the head, and the player must face the throw direction. Note also the feet for both throw cases: (1) directly in front and (2) at an angle to the touch-line.

1. One or both feet are off the ground at the time of the throw.
2. The player favors one hand during the throw. This is apparent when the ball in flight is spinning.
3. The body is not facing the field.
4. Not starting the ball from behind the head.
5. Releasing the ball before it passes the face.

Care should be made to maintain ball possession during a throw-in. If throw-ins are not taken seriously enough, the opposition will end up with the ball after one, two, or even five of your players have touched the ball. Carefully watch throw-ins to see which team actually ends up with the ball at the outcome of the throw-in. Your team may be turning over the ball more frequently than you realize. In a game of ball possession, each possessive play increases your chances of winning.

It is essential that your players know that the ball should always go to an open player. This means that throwing the ball "up the line" is just about the last place to throw because opponents always seem to congregate there. The players must move around to get open or draw off players to enable another teammate to become open for this pass. The throw can be made to the goalkeeper or to another player who shields the ball and immediately passes it back to the thrower. The throw must be made in such a way that the receiver can control the ball or head it back to the thrower's feet. Naturally, these routine plays must be practiced often. Throw-in drills are outlined in Chapter 6.

There is one final note on throw-ins. A throw-in is not valid unless it enters the field of play, and it is repeated by the same team if the ball does not go over the touch line after being thrown. Wind could cause such a condition. It should also be mentioned here that a player receiving the ball cannot be offside on a throw-in.

4. Elements of the Game

Players

This section is geared more toward coaches of younger teams who need a quick understanding of player characteristics, but experienced coaches may find the observations about positions interesting and possibly useful.

There are some players who will learn more skills than others; these players can be considered generalists. The players who only learn certain skills and employ only these skills can be considered specialists. The reason for grouping these players into categories is to help coaches place players in their best positions. Both generalists and specialists are needed to form a strong team, and the following categories can help identify them. The outside midfielders fall between specialists and generalists. The sweeper back and the center half backs would be considered generalists. The stopper back, the wing defenders, and the forwards are considered specialists, while the goalkeeper seems to fit into both categories.

Players can be further typed by observing certain characteristics. Defense people generally are tough, both mentally and physically. Forwards are generally trim individuals who seek glamour. Midfielders are generally a cross between being somewhat aggressive and somewhat shy. Goalkeepers are often just different. Whatever the player's characteristics and skills are, it is important to remind coaches that weaker players should not be placed into defensive positions.

In general, the right and left sides of the field are symmetrical, and the right and left player positions can be treated equally. The right and left attacking wing positions may be treated slightly differently, however, because most players prefer kicking with either their right or left foot. This makes a difference at the forward wing positions. While soccer players are encouraged to learn to kick with either foot, not all players become adept with both feet. It is often said that a good player should be able to play all positions, but this is only true to a point. I believe that there are one or two positions that are best suited for most players. It is up to the coach to experiment with players to match them up with their optimum position or positions.

GOALKEEPER

This person is usually a different type of soccer player. His one strong characteristic may be his confidence in himself. Confident goalkeepers usually gain the respect of players of both teams. A confident goalkeeper can "psyche" opponents with his prowess. Goalkeepers usually have a desire and drive to be different from others. This is obvious when one considers that this person generally does not play soccer in the same manner as the rest of the team. And this attribute of wanting to be different can produce a strong defensive leader. His specialty is, of course, defending the goal. This person is also a generalist because he must learn to be in control of the defense but have the skill to start effective attacks.

CENTER DEFENSE PERSON

Often these players are physically strong and self-confident. They may not possess an array of soccer skills but are keen at reading play build-ups by the opposition. The best center defense people seem to be more defense-minded with less of a desire to work on attack build-ups for their own team; they seem to have a desire to destroy attacks by the opposition. Advanced center defense players should have a strong theoretical knowledge of all of the finer points of soccer to understand attacking strategies. They are specialists because their main task is to break up attacks or "stop-up" the center of the defense line.

SWEEPER BACK

This person must be able to read attacking plays and observe weaknesses in her own defense. She must be able to "float" in the defensive area while defending against an attack. This person is a generalist because she does not have a specific area to cover but must constantly be observing what is going on and must also take part in the attacks. This person should develop a good theoretical knowledge of the game and should learn to be very skillful with the head and feet. Not only should a sweeper back be able to break up attacks, but she should also be able to start ground attacks by settling air balls or receiving passes from the goalkeeper. Often this person will dribble the ball halfway up the field without opposition because she may not be marked by an opponent. This player must have the ability to recover to the defense after having gone forward on an attack.

DEFENSIVE WINGERS

These players may not be as strongly built as the center defensive players, but they are more defense-minded than attack-oriented players. They should be fast and alert. They may not possess a full knowledge of the finer points of soccer and may not possess a full array of skills. They should be highly intelligent, however, as they should have a full knowledge of attack strategies. They must be self-disciplined and should be able to employ this knowledge during game pressure because a single mistake by either of the defensive wingers could cost you the game. Several mistakes by these players will almost always cost you the game. They are specialists because their main job is to neutralize attacking wingers by always being goalside of their opponent. These players are not usually noticed because most of the eyes are on the attackers. The defensive wingers may not have much contact with the ball during attacks on either side, but they can perform their job correctly by completely neutralizing the wing attacker during the entire game. This type of performance can be beautiful if one knows what to look for.

CENTER HALFBACKS

The duties of the center half backs are described only for the three recommended formations for youth soccer. Depending on the formation, one to four center half backs may be used. When employing the W-M formation, four half backs are used — two attack-minded forward half backs and two defense-minded rear half backs. When four center half backs required for the W-M formation are used, the mental and physical duties normally performed by a single center half back of the 4-3-3 and the 3-3-4 formation will be split up among them.

The forward half backs should be able to work together with the forward line for attacking, and the rear half backs should be more defensive by being play-destroy oriented and aggressive, but they are possibly the least skillful of the half backs. When one center half back is used, he has the responsibility of overseeing all the surrounding players; young players are excluded here. The center half back is often the captain of the team. This position requires a generalist, while the four half backs used in the W-M formation would be specialists.

The best person for the position of center half back is one who is field smart, level-headed, and skillful, with a knowledge of the finer points of soccer. This person should also be high-spirited and persistent, with a high energy level. Feeding the ball to unmarked teammates is paramount to other offensive functions. This player should be observed to have a desire to win loose balls, bring them under control, and then start ground attacks by feeding controllable-balls out to the forward wings. This player must have the energy to roam up and down the field and to assure that no midfield gap remains open, especially for defensive reasons. This player must be adept and give commands to the team, chiefly to the midfield and forward players. This player must be sufficiently skillful to do the jobs of the other players that he oversees.

WING HALFBACKS

When there are three half backs, there are two wing half backs — one on each wing. These players are offensive play-formers as well as defensive play-destroyers. Their job is to be constantly feeding the ball to forward players on offense as well as to cover the midfield wings for defense. They may also overlap the forward wings and temporarily replace these wing players in time of attack. They generally do not need a strong knowledge of the game to play this position, but they should know enough to recover to their position after an assault on the opponent's goal has subsided. They do need endurance because they must be constantly running up and down the field, especially if they fully support frontal attacks on goal. It should be noted that if a weaker player is substituted here, it is important to back this person with a strong defense person.

RIGHT AND LEFT FORWARD WINGERS

These players should be extremely fast while dribbling the ball. They are specialists because their main function is to assist in scoring or actually scoring. One of their main functions is to cross the ball in front of the goal, out of the goalkeeper's defensive range. Another important function is to follow up on shots taken by other forwards (not hanging back). Often shots on goal that come from the right wing (or left wing) miss the goal and pass in front of the opposite side of the goal. The ball may also be deflected in this direction by the goalkeeper. When this player performs her job correctly, she will fully support the attack without getting into an offside position. The ball, however, may not often come within reach of this player.

It is often said that a right footer should play the right wing and a left footer should play the left wing. If this is the case, then these players must make blind crosses to cross the ball to the center of the goal. This effective blind cross is discussed in Chapter 6, but it is not as effective as a nonblind cross. This is why it is actually more advantageous to place a left-footed kicker on the right wing and vice versa. It is better to make crosses while the player has vision of the goal and the potential receiver, and this is not usually the case when making the blind cross kick.

The visual cross (the nonblind cross) permits the receiver to be within the kicker's line of vision at the time of the kick, but the blind cross is made with the kicker's vision of the receiver obscured. The nonblind kick is made by the right foot from the left wing by the player making approximately a 45-degree angle cut-in towards the goal after dribbling up the left wing. On the one hand, from the left wing, using the right foot and the instep kick, the kicker has the receiver in view (not at the instant of a properly performed kick, however). If on the other hand, the player is a left-footed kicker on the left wing, she must dribble the ball up the left wing towards the corner flag. Several feet from the flag, the kick must be made, and the kicker must "pull" the ball back to place it out of reach of the goalkeeper's hands; this kick is done blindly. One might ask why this player is not instructed to also cut in at the same 45-degree angle when kicking with the left foot from the left wing. The reason is that it is very difficult to cut inward from the left wing and "pull" the ball backwards using the instep kick with the left foot and vice versa. Furthermore, it must be noted that amateur players seldom make good crosses anyway. This is because players have a lack of training and knowledge in this area.

CENTER FORWARDS

These players are specialists and often do not need a full array of soccer skills. They should be aware that opponent defense people often try to intimidate them. They should possess good heading and trapping skills under pressure. They must be able to go rapidly through the moves to get off shots on goal properly and accurately. Height or a strong build will give them a slight advantage in heading and will help intimidate the opposition. These individuals are normally not defense-oriented and prefer this glamorous position: usually these players like to score goals more then they like team playing. If the center forward is not scoring goals, this individual should be removed or placed in another location, unless he is not being fed passes by the midfielders and wingers. In this case it is the others who are not doing their job well. If the center forward is frequently setting up plays for others, he would best be placed in the midfield or forward wing position.

Soccer Formations

Before introducing a few useful formations, it is necessary to emphasize that an overall plan be developed and followed before employing the new techniques. Often coaches switch to different styles of play because they are not getting the desired performance from their present methods and are losing games. Changing a formation could be the correct action, but this must be resolved in practices first, not on the spur of the moment while losing a game. Coaches sometimes decide to change formations and issue special instructions to players to counteract strong opposition players. Naturally, these coaches assume that these instructions can be and will be carried out. Reality does not work this way, however. Unless the players have practiced the new formation, they will often get into a state of consternation. Players cannot play optimally under these conditions. The situation further deteriorates when the coach says, "Go back and play in the original formation." Some credibility must be lost here. So before you decide to change formation, choose a plan and stick with it. This plan should incorporate the players' strengths and weaknesses. This analysis may show that there is no single center half back player. Instead, there may be five or six available players who could be effectively utilized as half backs employing the W-M formation. It should be noted in regard to the above discussion that a coach could train the team to have alternate plans and formations.

When any formation is utilized, each player, especially a specialist, must be taught what her role is in the overall team picture. Each player has a job on both attack and defense. The following are but a few examples where players hurt the team and reduce the team's chance of winning: (1) when a defender goes forward on attack but cannot recover sufficiently fast to defend properly, (2) when the center halfback settles the ball and dribbles it up the center of the field without passing it to an open player for a consolidated team attack, (3) when a half back cannot participate in all attacks and does not pick up an opposing player when the opposition is in possession of the ball, (4) when the goalkeeper continually kicks the ball up-field and takes her time to get the ball to a player, and (5) when the goalkeeper permits another player to take the goal-kicks. In the latter case there are effectively 9 receiving players to 11 opposing players.

In summary, for each style of play, what is to be expected and what is not to be expected must be conveyed to all players. If players go out on the soccer field and play a position without a coach's explanation, the goalkeeper may think that she just catches and kicks the ball, the defenders may think that it is enough just to kick the ball up to the forward players to score, and the midfielders may think that they are just supposed to run up the field to follow the ball. This type of play is pure kickball, and kickball is not what is being practiced. If the coach firmly believes in a new and better approach, a commitment should be made to develop a new team strategy simply because the present one is not effective. Each player should know her present role. This is also important when substituting a player. It is best to explain the person's duties in terms of how she is to support the

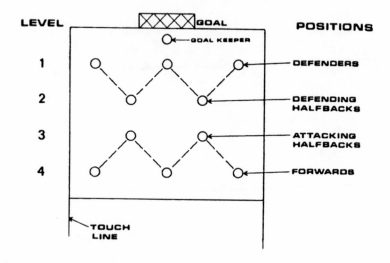

Figure 4-1. The W-M formation. Note that this formation has four levels of players.

team rather than stating, "You are going in as a fullback, so hustle to the ball."

The following formations are discussed on the basis of defense and winning strategy.

W-M FORMATION

This is an old formation, but it is an especially useful one for younger soccer teams that have an excess of good half backs. This formation, unlike the others discussed, has four levels instead of three. It has two forward half backs and two defensive half backs. The W-M formation is shown in Fig. 4-1. The forward half backs are more oriented towards ball control and for setting up plays for the forward players. The rear half backs are more oriented towards play-destroying and should be fast players. As mentioned earlier, these players may not be as skillful at ball handling as their more forward counterparts, but they should be scrappers who like to get in where the action is and stir things up. One of the advantages of this formation is that the midfielders do not have as much ground to cover and do not burn up as much energy as midfielders in a three-tier system. This four-level

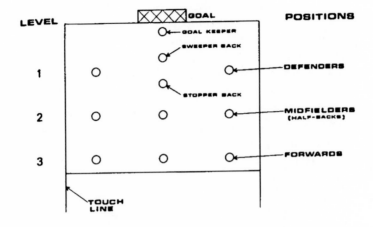

Figure 4-2. The 4-3-3 formation. Note that the sweeper back adds support to the defense in the event that there is an unmarked opponent.

formation helps prevent midfield gaps that often occur when a single center half back does not maintain control over the midfield. As is often stated, when the team loses control over the midfield, it has lost control of the game.

A slight drawback of this formation is that one does not have a team leader in the key position of center half back. This is not important with younger teams, however, because in youth soccer the captain of the team usually does not do more then call heads or tails in the coin flip at kickoff time.

4-3-3 FORMATION

This formation utilizes a sweeper, two wing defenders, and a stopper back in the defense, a center half back, two wing half backs, a center forward, and two attacking wing players. (See Fig. 4-2.) This formation gives the team a strong defense. The wing defenders must watch the opposing attacking wingers closely. As these attacking wingers penetrate into your defensive area, they must be closely marked. If an opposing winger gets closer to your defending goal than your defending winger, the latter player is out of position. The defensive wingers, as well as the stopper back, must always be goalside of the attacker in their zone. If any opponent gets through the defense, the sweeper back must tightly mark this person.

In this formation, your attacking strategy should be as follows: since attacks from the defense can start anywhere, any player who has the ball, including the goalkeeper, should look for an open teammate on the wings to continue the attack. The ball should not be passed to the stopper or sweeper when they are in the center near your own goal unless this player is completely unmarked. A passing or trapping mistake can cost you a goal.

With this formation, the center half back must control the game. He must be able to have total ball control and continuously look for unmarked teammates, especially on the wings. On defense, he must be able to pick up an opponent dribbling the ball through the center of the field, read the plays that are starting against his team, win a loose ball, settle it, and pass it to an unmarked teammate. Heading the ball up-field or flicking it up-field with the head or foot is a kickball tactic and indicates that this player should be removed. To some people, a player putting the ball generally over or through the opposition defense may look good, but this is usually a nonconstructive move, even if a anomalous goal is scored. Only a conscious pass to an open player with the ability to control it is a good pass. This player is doing his job properly if he makes good, short, controllable passes that can be utilized. With good center half back available, this can be an ideal formation.

3-3-4 FORMATION

This formation is a variation of the 4-3-3 formation. Instead of employing a sweeper back as an extra measure of defense, the extra player is another center forward. This is a good formation for very young players because the inexperienced players usually cannot think sufficiently to be effective sweeper backs. It is still a defensive formation because it incorporates three midfielders and three defenders. With young players, goals are often scored by players rushing at the goal as in kickball, so when utilizing this formation, you must insist that your players immediately return to their defensive zones while under attack. This formation is the least complex and the most manageable by coaches of very young teams.

4-4-2 FORMATION

This formation is a variation of the 4-2-4 formation, which is not discussed. It is a strongly defensive system in which the left and right wingers are moved back to be the left and right wing half backs. In defense, the four midfielders are backed up by four defenders, making it difficult to score against the formation when proper defensive tactics are adhered to. The two center forwards should be specialists. They should be strong, powerful, and preferably tall. They are up front mainly for scoring and generally do not make plays, but they should apply pressure on the defense and draw off opposition players at critical times. The two wing midfielders become attacking wingers when their team has possession of the ball. This formation is not recommended for youth soccer because the two center forwards are complete specialists and may not show up at games for some reason. It is difficult to replace these players, who must be experienced in this role and must know how to work in unison with each other.

3-2-5 FORMATION

In youth soccer, many coaches experiment with different formations. Probably the most outdated formation is the 3-2-5 system. This system uses three defensive players, two midfield players, and five attacking forwards. The problems with this system when playing modern controlled-ball soccer are the following:

1. The system carries the assumption that five attackers increase the goal-scoring chances. Coaches employing this formation also underestimate the need for the remaining six players to help in the attack. The system also underestimates the opponent's defensive capabilities and the need for another one or two defenders when one's own goal is being counterattacked.

2. The system gives the team an unbalanced workload. The two midfielders have to cover the area from penalty area to penalty area. The five forwards basically attack when they get the ball and hang around the halfline when the ball is in their own defensive area. The three defenders are usually too overworked to help out effectively in an attack, so they usually just boot the ball up-field or over the touch line.

3. The system polarizes the team into specialties such as defenders, attackers, and midfielders.

General Attacking and Defending

It is truly said that when your team has the ball, the whole team is on the attack. This means that every field player should be moving forward when you have possession of the ball. In addition, players without the ball should be moving into open space for a pass or to draw out opponents. If teammates do not do this continually, it makes it harder for the player carrying the ball to decide to whom she should pass. If many of your players are near the ball, you can be sure that they will be drawing the opponents with them toward the ball, thus limiting the empty space into which the ball carrier can dribble and reducing the chances that the ball carrier will have an open player to pass to. Smart players "off the ball" draw players out, away from the attacking goal, giving the whole team a better chance to score. This tactic of drawing players, say toward the wings, removes chokes around the opponents' goal. The closer that you are to this goal, the less space you will have because the goal acts like a funnel. Defenders can form a defensive "fence" surrounding this funnel, which is often very difficult to penetrate because of the offside law. When opponent defenders are choking up their defending goal, ball control and the drawing away of defenders are necessary to improve your chances of scoring. This is far superior to just indiscriminately kicking the ball up-field, unless your team just overpowers the other team. Ball control gives you the competitive edge if you are closely matched. If your team is much more powerful than the opposition, then any style of play will do. But practicing ball control against a weak team prepares you for the next tough match.

One element of uncontrolled soccer playing, or kickball is worth mentioning. When playing kickball, the goalie or a defender boots the ball up-field to the attackers. There is about a 30 to 40 percent chance that your team will recover it, mainly because the opposition players are facing the ball and this makes it is a lot easier to settle it.

In comparison with kickball, in which there is no clue of a plan, an ideal attack using a 4-3-3 formation may take place from the kickoff as follows. The start whistle has blown, and the ball is kicked off. The forward receiving the kicked-off ball should immediately pass it back to the center half back, who in turn should pass the ball out on the ground to a wing half back. The attacking winger on the same side of the field should accelerate up-field along the touch line to receive a pass. Ideally, this player has space to dribble the ball up that wing. The whole team should be moving up-field supporting the attack. The winger has these options: (1) Cross the ball to the penalty spot in front of the goal or to any open player in front of the goal. (2) Change fields by making an air pass across the field to the other winger. (3) Pass the ball back to the half back winger, who then overtakes the original winger (the one who made that pass-back). This receiver now becomes a temporary winger, and the forward player hangs back as the temporary half back winger or moves in towards the center of the field for a possible chance at a shot on goal. This possession game up-field should be continued until the opponent's defense makes a mistake and one of your attackers gets a chance at scoring. During all of this activity, players must be careful not to become offside. (See Law XI on page 186, "Off-Side.")

In another situation, an attack is started by the goalkeeper, who immediately makes a thrown ground pass to the wing defender, if that player is unmarked. If it becomes apparent that the receiver is in danger of being overpowered by an opponent, the goalkeeper should call for the ball to be returned immediately. It is hoped that the goalkeeper will find another player open for a safe pass. At this time, all time advantage has been lost, and the goalkeeper may find no alternative but to kick the ball up-field, but it should be sent towards the wings. A short kick, on the ground if possible, to the wing half back may immediately start another counterattack on the goal. A comment is worth mentioning about the wing pass. There is usually more space available to settle the ball out at the wings than there is in the middle of the field. This type of attacking strategy should be employed whenever any attack starts in the rear of the midfield or back line; the rearward player receiving the ball should settle it quickly and then quickly pass it on the ground, if possible, to any open wing player.

The following situation occurs frequently enough in soccer to merit consideration. A fast, aggressive player dribbles the ball up the center of the field from some midfield point. This player dribbles up-field and is unassisted by any teammates. Near the opponent's goal, however, defenders begin to converge on him as he continues towards the goal. Often this player has supporting teammates, especially to the rear. This player continues towards the goal even though there is little chance that he will get off a good shot on goal. The defenders converge

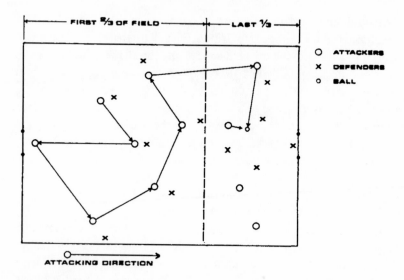

Figure 4-3. An ideal attack. Note carefully the direction of the ball. Upon receiving each pass, the O-team player places his back to the X-team player to shield the ball, being careful not to obstruct the opponent.

on the attacking player and succeed in easily taking the ball away from him. Such situations usually amount to a fruitless effort, but could be advantageous if this player utilized his team. Scoring chances are few, so do not waste them. In tough games, unassisted scoring of this type rarely occurs. This situation should not be confused with one in which a breakaway player is one-on-one against the goalkeeper.

Any attack may not go ideally as planned because of defensive resistance, but the various methods of attack should be impressed upon the team. Controlled ball soccer is not a game where players run around haphazardly in order to score — it is a game utilizing continuous zigzag ground passing. Fig. 4-3 shows an ideal passing situation. The ball is only passed to an open teammate, that is, a teammate who has an opponent behind him. If a teammate has an opponent to his side, then the player with the ball should look for an unmarked teammate to make the pass to. These teammates should not be too difficult to locate in your own ⅔ of the field, unless the opponents are tightly marking your players. The following rules should be insisted upon when launching attacks or breaking up opposing attacks to regain possession of the ball.

Rule 1: The ball must be trapped stationary at the feet; when your team has the ball, the whole team is on the attack.

Rule 2: Short, no-risk ground passes are made in any direction in the following manner:

A. Keep the ball on the ground as much as possible.

B. Passes should be not less than 5' (1 ½ meters) nor more than 30' (9 meters) in the first ⅔ of the field (your defending portion of the field).

Note carefully the direction of the ball in the figure; each pass cannot be intercepted by an X-player because of shielding. Care must be used not to cause an obstruction. The goalkeeper should also be used.

Rule 3: Each player must be able to carry the ball (dribble and shield the ball).

Rule 4: When receiving the ball near an opposing player, the trapper must turn her back to the opponent who is putting pressure on her as soon as the ball is contacted and shield the ball with her body. This makes trapping under pressure relatively easy. See "shielding immediately upon receiving the ball" in Chapter 3.

Rule 5: When entering the last ⅓ of the field, the pressure becomes greater, space becomes limited, the opponent density becomes greater, their security is being attacked, and they play harder. Your aim is to funnel the ball into 24' (7 ½ meters) of the goal, while their aim is just to clear the ball out in about any direction. This means that in this zone your players must make careful passes or placements of the ball to certain areas such as shown in Fig. 4-4. The attacking winger, if located in the position shown in the figure, should place the ball (filled circle) towards one of the lettered circles. Long once-on shots and small angle shots on goal should be discouraged. They seldom go into the goal. Most of these shots are saved by the goalkeeper, and the team's effort is wasted.

Rule 6: When your team has lost the ball, the forwards must now each pick up an opposing defender "person-to-person" (formerly called man-to-man). In this way the opposition has no open players to pass to and is forced into making mistakes. When the opposition reaches your defending ⅓ of the field, the defense goes back to zone defense.

Rule 7: Defenders are all players when the opposition has possession of the ball. The defender with the opponent dribbling the ball must back up with this player and continue to back up with the opponent without moving towards the ball. Only when the dribbler has lost control of the ball should the defender go for the ball. In order for soccer players to be able to perform their team duties correctly, they must be in top condition. For this end, the coaches must give all players rigorous training, including much running. It is also up to each player to maintain his endurance with

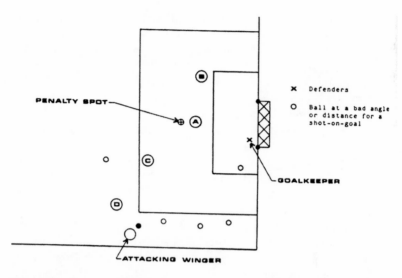

Figure 4-4. Direct shots taken from small angles or long distances as shown seldom amount to a goal. It is best for a player to aim at "A" or "B" in the air or on the ground, or on the ground to position "C" or "D." Naturally teammates are at these places.

supplementary self-conditioning; it must be remembered that players in top condition are less prone to injury then players playing a sport beyond their limitations. In addition, as a precautionary measure, prior to the training season, both players and trainers should consult a physician.

Defensive Strategy

Defensive strategy can be considered one of the most important principles in winning games against strong competitive teams. It is far easier to plan to prevent goals by the opposition than to plan to score goals against their unknown defense. Since outdoor soccer is a game in which the losing team almost never gets three goals and possibly gets one or two goals, the defense can be a vital part of the strategy. The score for competitive soccer is ordinarily so low that letting in one or two goals can produce decisive victory against you. Errors that are made by your forwards may not be too significant, but one or two defensive errors can be costly. Defensive strategy does not mean, however, that if your team scores first, you protect this lead and play without offense the rest of the game.

The defensive strategy starts when each team member picks up an opposing player when the team is without the ball, except when the ball is in your own defensive area. Here the defenders should probably play zonal defense, although your forwards and midfielders must each tightly cover an opponent. This will not happen, though, if players are not in excellent physical condition. This pressure is extremely useful when containing the ball in the opponent's defensive area because less energy is expended for your counterattacks. It might be expected that the opposition defense will make several mistakes because often they do not possess the ball control skills that up-field players do. This pressure also helps the midfield to remain organized.

As stated earlier in this chapter, if there is no pressure on the opposing defensive players by your forwards, your midfield will probably be scrambling about trying to cover too much ground. If the midfield is scrambling about, the defense usually becomes disorganized. When the defensive line is confused or disorganized, a tactical error could cost you the game. An important factor in all of this defensive pressure is the conservation of energy for your attacks. By applying constant pressure, your forwards should start their attacks on goal from shorter distances. This is highly desirable because that energy ordinarily expended by players bringing the ball from one defensive end to the other can now be better utilized by making quicker moves when they get near the opponent's goal.

To get a handle on your team's effectiveness for repelling the opponents, it is important to observe from where most of the opposing team's attacks are launched. If they originate in the midfield, either your forwards are not applying pressure, your center half back or halfbacks are not playing effectively, or both. If most of their attacks originate from between the halfline and your defensive zone, your team is in trouble. At this point, a midfield or forward substitution or two should be considered, along with reminders passed to all players that they must pressure the other team.

THE GOALKEEPER'S ROLE

The key responsibility for defensive strategy for the back defensive line lies with your goalkeeper. This player is in a key position because all players are always within her view. If this person is technically skillful, she will gain the respect of the other teammates. This is done not by making friends with the defensive players, but rather by concentrating on maintaining control of these same players for the purpose of protecting the goal. She should never let herself go unprotected.

The goalkeeper must be commanding the players at all times as she deems necessary, but in a quiet manner. It is important that this player assure that her teammates are watching their opposition person in their defensive area and are not vulnerable because they are watching only the ball. It is normal that when the goalkeeper wants the ball, she shouts "goalkeeper." And this additional responsibility of being in charge of the defense is a tall order for any person to fulfill, so it will not ordinarily come early in one's career. With the younger teams, if coaching from the sidelines is permitted, a coach should fulfill this role and instruct the goalkeeper that he is substituting for this aspect of the goalkeeper's job.

As mentioned many times before, the defender must not go for the ball unless the dribbler has lost control of it. The goalkeeper must always be on the alert for this possibility and should also be aware that there should be no slide tackling near the goal. When this occurs and the ball is missed, the defender is now out of position. In fact, this is the worst position for a defender to be in. This player may be on the ground while the attacker may have a shot on goal opposed only by the goalkeeper. If a defender commits a serious mistake and no goal is scored, the incident should be treated as severely as if a goal had been scored. If this is not done, the mistake will undoubtedly be repeated.

When there is an attack mounted against your goal, each person's defensive territory is shrinking. This causes a defensive line to form a tight ring around the goal. The defense will eventually come to a halt. If there is a now shot on goal and each defense person is in place, there is an excellent chance that the goalkeeper can anticipate the opponent's placement of the ball. If a defender gets out of position, however, it is anyone's guess where the shot will be aimed.

A fairly common expression in soccer is "the goalkeeper is the first one on the attack." This is true only if the goalkeeper gets the ball to a teammate who can effectively control it. Part of defensive strategy is ball possession. Obviously, when one has ball possession, there is no need for defense. This is then the goalkeeper's first line of defense; that is, keeping the ball out of his territory and with his own team is the optimum defensive measure. The best place to start an attack is out at the wings. This can be effective only when the ball is placed back into play immediately. The defense people, of course, must anticipate this strategy. As stated before, field players should be discouraged from taking the goal kicks because this tactic reduces your eligible receivers to 9, while there are 11 eligible opposing players as potential receivers.

Attack Soccer vs. Defensive Soccer

When a coach places too much emphasis on the techniques for goal scoring, he is not giving enough thought to the big picture of the game. This is attack soccer. Attack soccer is soccer at a very elementary level. Young teams have weak defense strategies, and this type of play can be effective here. This all changes, however, as the teams progress on up in age. Even with nondisciplined older teams, this type of playing is often utilized when a team is down by at least one goal. Players revert to nondisciplined type of play when they start placing "through balls" into the opponent's defense in attempt to allow the forwards to score or when a single player tries to score all by himself. This is generally a nondisciplined form of play and cannot compete well against more disciplined, skillful play in which the players rely more heavily on ball control.

When a coach meshes the individual functions of each player into a team unit, he is probably using defensive strategy. When attacking players can rely on others to do their jobs correctly, they can concentrate on their own jobs and should score more frequently. Goals generally follow when the defensive players and their teammates are performing their jobs correctly. This, of course, can only happen if forward (and sometimes midfield players) have some abilities for scoring. In defensive soccer, players pressure opponents in possession of the ball into making mistakes. This style of play occurs when your players back up with these ball-possessing opponents and when your players pass the ball back and forth to prevent the opponents from getting it themselves. This type of control-ball play is so effective that some top professional teams that historically played the long-ball style of play switched to the short-ball style of play shortly after being outplayed by some of the teams concentrating on ball control.

The short-ball style of play is more technical and demands self-disciplined shielding that goes with trapping the ball at the feet. The long-ball style of play does not require too much in the way of ball control disciplines. It relies more on powerful long kicks and long headers up field. It also is not very effective against a strong defense and is generally obsolete in high level competition.

BALL CONTROL

Ball control is the most elementary offensive technique, and each player should endeavor to master it. In order for a player to approach professionalism, that player needs to master self-control and ball control, the conscious ability to get the ball from point A to point B, to a teammate, or into the goal. Ball control starts with shielding the ball with the body while moving or looking around for the best opportunity. If a player does not learn to shield the ball immediately upon receiving it or while possessing it, she will not advance in this sport. This is important for goalkeepers to comprehend when they are launching an attack.

Ball control, along with defensive strategy, endurance, and the never-quitting spirit, builds winning teams. If you are the first coach to promote this type of play to the players of a team, you may not have an immediate success story. If you coach this same group of individuals in the following years, you may still not have a championship team. You will have, however, the feeling that you have helped create a team that plays together and create players who have gained self-confidence and skills to play in higher competitive teams. You may also win a few future championships. If you do not find that skillful play enables you to beat all other teams that you play against, it may be for these reasons: teams that play a rough game of kickball can intimidate your players with their roughness or they may just "out-hustle" your players to the ball. They may also have a slightly older team. If the skilled style of play is not adequate to produce sufficient wins, your players may be nonaggressive. The shoulder-charging-tackle drill in Chapter 7 may provide that needed difference. Also giving an explanation on Law XII, paragraph (e), which states that a player may not charge an opponent from behind "unless the latter is obstructing [the ball]," should prepare the players for the allowed roughness in soccer.

Plays

Plays in soccer, especially in youth soccer, usually involve no more than one or two players, with only a few touches on the ball. There is one main exception, and that exception is on a kickoff, discussed below. In general, though, plays in soccer should not be confused with planned plays in other sports; with a few exceptions, the dynamic plays are spontaneous as they unfold when an instantaneous set of field conditions becomes just right. Some of the more common plays are throw-ins where the ball is returned to the thrower, the wall pass, kicks around or through a wall, crossing and passing the ball to a player for a shot on goal (trapping in front of the goal), and corner kicks. Some of these plays are discussed below.

KICKOFF

The ball is not in play until it has moved forward and has gone the distance of its circumference, according to Law VIII. The player taking the kickoff cannot touch the ball until it has been touched by another player. Probably the best offensive play on a kickoff is to have the first receiver pass the ball back immediately to the center half back or a wing half back. With one of the half backs now in possession of the ball, it is advisable to utilize one of the wing players along the touch line as the next receiver. This wing player can then carry the ball up the touch line and make a cross to the forwards following up the attack. This is a full play using several players and can be practiced as a training exercise. The method is similar to an attack down the wing as discussed above in "General Attacking and Defending."

The loss of about 10 yards (9 meters) on the kickoff is insignificant. Trying to gain yardage on the kickoff is not advisable because all territory up-field is very adequately covered by opponents. Modern soccer requires ball possession, and by not following the above

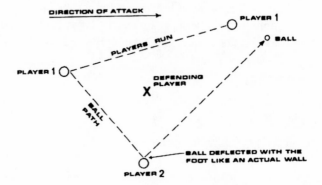

Figure 4-5. The wall pass against one defender. Note that the ball should end up in front of the feet of the initial ball carrier, player 1.

strategy, a team can easily risk losing the ball. Naturally, anomalies do occur, especially in young age soccer. A goal that is scored immediately as a result of moving directly forward after a kickoff may cause one to believe that this should be the norm. This type of play will usually result, however, in the loss of the ball almost at once or several touches later.

WALL PASS

This play, the wall pass (also known as "give and go"), gets its name because one player that must use his foot as a wall. The "wall" is used to deflect the ball back to the original player as this player moves up-field. It is used to pass an opponent utilizing a two player to one player advantage. This technique is illustrated in Fig. 4-5. This play is carried out as follows:

Player 1 may be dribbling the ball up-field and approaches defending player X (opponent). Player 1 wishes to go by X so he shoots a pass to player 2. Player 2 does not trap the ball, but instead deflects the ball with his foot so it ends up in front of player 1. Player 1 approaches the ball, touches it, to regain control of it and maintains his stride up field. The result is that player 1 has passed opponent X.

Note 1: This play must be practiced with an actual opponent or with a field marker substituting for the defender.

Note 2: This play is definitely not recommended for young players.

If they learn to use this play and have not mastered shielding and trapping, they will often substitute the above moves for ball control simply because it is easier to deflect the ball then to control it under pressure situations. In addition, it may not at first seem so, but this play consists of a set of precise movements. Without the precision needed to complete the play successfully, the ball can easily change teams as the result of a mistake.

DEFENSIVE PLAY ON THROW-INS

By applying pressure to the opposition during their throw-ins, your team can frequently regain possession of the ball. This is especially effective in youth soccer, where the opponents may neglect this area of playing. Defensive play on opponent's throw-ins is accomplished by marking every opponent within throwing distance. Place an extra one or two players "down the line" (the opponent's up-field side near the touch line). Each of your players must mark one and only one opponent by standing behind him. These players are to remain behind their opponent until the play is over. The play is not over until the ball is out of the area. Any of your nearby players standing in an open area are not helping out.

Always observe which team ends up with the ball on a throw-in. It is important to do this when both sides are taking the throw-ins. The results are determined only after there have been several touches on the ball and it is clear who has gained possession of it. Observe what strategies took place to produce the end result. This type of observation should also take place on goal kicks and with kicks resulting from penalties because scoring in well-played competition is a function of ball possession and the team that has the most ball possession time is generally the team that ends up with the most goals.

CROSSES FOR SHOTS ON GOAL

Crosses are used very often for the purpose of scoring, but the younger the soccer age, the less effective they are. In fact, amateurs seldom make effective crosses for a variety of reasons. The cross is frequently directed exactly to the goalkeeper or made too near the near goalpost to be useful. The cross must be out of the goalkeeper's reach (outside of the goal area). This technique is described in the "Blind Cross Kick," see Chapter 7. There are other problems that occur with crosses received by young players. Even if the ball is perfectly placed in the air, these players generally do not have the skill to head it properly. And when the ball arrives in the proper place on the ground for a once-on type of kick, very often the player will look up at the goalkeeper instead of at the ball at the time of the shot, thus sacrificing accuracy. And finally, another problem is that players generally are not proficient in trapping and getting the shot off quickly. The drills for this method of shooting on goal, the trap and shoot drills, and other crossing drills are described in Chapter 6.

Blind crosses should be made to the penalty spot, when kicked in the air. If a more experienced player making the cross spots a player in front of the near or far post, he may endeavor to send the ball to this person's head. The near post is preferable because the ball does not cross in front of the goalkeeper. Nonblind crosses can be made using the variations of the instep kick while the player is coming toward the goal at some oblique angle to the goal line. These are more accurate because the receiver is in view prior to the instant that the kicker looks down at the ball. Crosses on the ground can be very effective if a defensive opponent is not directly in line with the kicker and receiver.

CORNER KICKS

A corner kick is taken by the attacking team when the defending team last touched the ball prior to it passing over the goal line outside of or over the goalpost. See Law XVII on page 192 for a more detailed explanation of corner kicks. Generally, the most effective type of corner kick is to place the ball in the air as described in the "Blind Cross Kick" section, providing it is not kicked directly into the goalkeeper's domain. Prior to the corner kick, the attacking team should be positioned about 20 yards (18 meters) from the goal area and start to move in just before the ball is kicked. If the attacking players are too close to the goal, the kicker will have a tendency to kick the ball close to the goalkeeper. Corner kicks should be practiced by having the forward players start their attack-on-goal well out into the field. They must learn to time their run to be at the penalty spot "line" (the 12-yard [11-meter] line in front of the goal) just as the ball arrives at this position. During games, it is a good idea to bring the two wing defenders up into position about halfway between the goal line and the halfline. Keep one defender on the halfline. After the second play on the ball, the wing defenders must recover to their zones so they will not get caught out of position if an opponent break-away occurs. The tactical reason for placing these wing defenders up front is to start another attack on goal, simply because the ball is defensively cleared into this area exceptionally often.

Short corner kicks are sometimes made to teammates near the kicking corner. After this has been done once, the next corner kick will have to be out to the goal area because opponents are now alerted to this type of play.

GOAL KICKS

A goal kick is given to the defending team when the attacking team last touched the ball before it passed over the goal line, that is, outside of or over the goalpost. The goal kick is taken from the goal area on the side of the field where the ball was in play prior to passing over the goal line. It is usually placed right on the goal area line, but it may be kicked from within the area. See Law XIV on page 190 for a more detailed explanation of the rules for goal kicks. Goal kicks are normally kicked far up-field to get the ball away from the defending goal. This is not always wise as this is not possession-ball soccer. If the ball is intercepted by an opponent, it may quickly return to your defending area.

Whenever possible, goal kicks should be taken by the goalkeeper because all potential receivers must be out in the field. The defensive wing should go out near the touch lines immediately when they observe the ball in the goalkeeper's hands. Other players should at once go to empty spaces to become potential receivers. The goalkeeper must immediately get the ball in play. Any delays only give the opposing players time to mark your players. The prime targets for the kick are the wing defenders. If the center-most players are unmarked, the ball could go to one of them next. This player in turn could play the ball once again, out to one of the wings to get the ball further up-field for a possible cross.

SHOT ON GOAL FOLLOW-UP

Often in games one can hear the coach say, "The ball is in front of the goal and there is no one there." Soccer players often do not press forward when a teammate comes within scoring distance of the goal. This reduces the chances for scoring goals. The shot taken by a teammate may be dropped by the goalkeeper, may be poorly kicked by a defender, or may cross laterally in front of the goal. If the left winger is taking the shot, the forward and right wing player should be in a nonoffside position but be supporting the player with the ball until the attack is definitely over.

FAKES

There are several feints or fakes that enable a player with the ball to deceive an opponent. These all take practice. The fakes can be practiced by players using any stationary object substituted for an opponent, such as a field marker, a tree, or a jacket. Coaches should encourage the use of fakes to promote self-confidence in players as they learn to control the ball.

Naturally, the feint is intended to deceive the opponent. In order to make the feint look convincing, the player must have full control of the ball near the feet. As she approaches the opponent and prepares to make the fake, she must slow down to have absolute control of the ball. There must be space on the side and rear of the opponent for the dribbler to maneuver into. The player executing a fake should only take on one opponent at a time.

The following fakes can be learned by young soccer players:

1. Feint to one side and go to the other side. This feint is useful when dribbling the ball up-field and approaching a lone opponent with space on, say, his right side and rear. Approach the opponent by slowing down to maintain ball control; the ball is pushed with every step. The ball and your feet must be in perfect synchronization. As you approach to within 10' (3 meters) of the opponent, feint to the left by placing the left foot toward his right side just as if you were going to run to this side. If this is convincing, the opponent will shift his weight to his right (your left), placing his balance on the right foot. Instead of continuing to your left, stop for an instant. Next, with the right foot trailing behind the left foot

and the ball in front of the right foot, push it with the outside of the right foot at about a 45-degree angle (on your right side) a few feet past him. With the opponent's balance still shifted to your left, you can pass the opponent to your right side and recover the ball. The 45-degree angle is critical. An angle less than 45 degrees may not allow sufficient room to pass him. An angle more than 45 degrees may give your opponent sufficient time and space to recover and prevent you from passing him. The speed of the kicked ball (at 45 degrees) must be fast enough to keep you from slowing down when recontacting the ball, yet slow enough for you to catch and control it before another opponent can reach it.

2. The fake through the opponent's legs. This may not exactly be a fake, but it falls into the general category because it is a technique to fool your opponent in order to pass him. Dribble the ball up to the opponent as if you wish to pass him, that is, slow down. If the opponent's legs are open and you think that you can reach the ball after your self-pass before anyone else will be able to reach it, use the push pass to accurately place the ball between his legs. Because of the opponent's inertia, you should be able to accelerate past him to reach and control the ball first.

3. Jumping over the stationary ball feint. This feint is used to give you room or time to pass when an opponent is marking you. Let us say, for example, that you are the right winger dribbling the ball up the right wing while being pursued by a defender. The defender manages to gets goalside of you, so you stop. The ball is now between the defender and you as he closes in on you. The defender waits for you to make your move but does not give you sufficient room to make a good pass and begins to come even closer to you. Keep the ball stationary in front of you. Then jump over the ball with only one foot exactly as if you were going to move with the ball in that direction. As the defender impulsively backs away, step back into your original starting position and make the pass (with more room then before). If no player is open for a pass, repeat this move. If this time the opponent does not "buy" this feint, you may have at least gained sufficient time to get teammates to come to your aid.

TRAPPING IN FRONT OF THE GOAL

It is very difficult to trap a ball at one's feet while under pressure, especially near the opponent's goal. But a skillful player on the front attacking line should be able to perform the correct moves to trap, shield, and shoot or pass. This sequence of events gives a player opportunities that would not be available otherwise. When taking a shot on goal, the following sequence should be mastered.

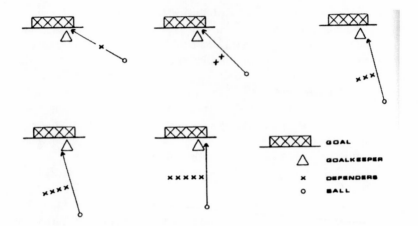

Figure 4-6. Setting up walls. Note that the goalkeeper sets up the wall to protect one side of the goal. Care should be taken to assure that the ball cannot be "bent" around the wall. An in-swinger kick could curve around the wall and go into the opposite side.

1. Go to the ball.
2. Stop before the ball contacts the foot.
3. Trap the ball at the feet (within 12 inches [.3 meter]) and shield it.
4. Look at the target.
5. Look down at the ball.
6. Position the ball with a slight push on it.
7. Get your balance.
8. Kick and follow through with the kick.
9. Then, and only then, look up.

This may sound complicated, but a skillful player will master all of the above steps and carry all of them out in a split second.

BREAK-AWAYS

The term *break-away* describes the event that occurs when a player with the ball breaks through the opposing defense and is all alone in front of the goalkeeper. This player may be closely followed by one or two defending opponents. If the player with the ball has sufficient time, she should choose a lower corner of the goal to shoot into if playing outdoor soccer and choose the upper corner if playing indoor soccer. The choice of left or right corner may best be made by observing the balance of the goalkeeper. If the balance is on one side, naturally the shot should be to the opposite side.

A player on a break-away should always think of the team before herself. When the opponents are closing in on this attacker and this player now has little or no room for a clear shot on goal, she must quickly decide on the options available to her. Often, when a player gets into this situation, the team has a much better chance of scoring a goal when the ball is passed back to an unmarked teammate. It should be kept in mind that defenders frequently will not give the attacking player an even chance to score. One or more of these players may use illegal tactics to keep this player from scoring.

Finally, this scenario can happen. A player is on a break-away with a seemingly clear shot on goal and kicks the ball wildly into the treetops over the goal. This may be the result of inexperience, opponent pressure, or anything else. It is not easy to concentrate on kicking the ball accurately while running at break-neck speed with opponents breathing down one's back and a confident looking goalkeeper facing one. To score goals, proper training is essential. Goal-scoring techniques must be practiced because only skillful training brings proficiency.

SETTING UP WALLS

The term *wall* describes one, two, or more players who stand together shoulder-to-shoulder facing the ball while protecting the groin area with their hands crossed. Walls are used by the defending team when they have committed a foul near their defending goal. The purpose of the wall is to form a shield against either a direct or indirect free kick. The shield of a player or players is constructed or "set up" 10 yards (9.15 meters) from the ball. The most useful method for setting up a wall is to skew the wall to one side of the goal while the goalkeeper attempts to cover the other side. See Fig. 4-6 for various arrangements of walls.

On an indirect kick, where the ball is placed on the ground closer than 10 yards (9.15 meters) to the goal, the players in the defensive wall will stand on the goal line inside of the goalposts. A goal may be directly scored on a direct free kick, but with an indirect free kick, it must touch another player prior to advancing beyond the goalposts for the goal to count. (See Law XIII on page 189.)

DRAWING OFF PLAYERS

This subject has been mentioned several times throughout this book. Drawing off players is an important aspect of team work needed to augment the team play. Players should be continuously working all the time while on the playing field. On the one hand, when a teammate has the ball and another player is within several yards (meters) of the player with the ball, it can be assumed, most of the time that he will be accompanied by an opponent. When this occurs with other teammates, there will be an overwhelming number of opponents near the ball. This is not a good situation because it will be difficult for your team to retain ball possession. On the other hand, when players move away from the ball, they will be drawing opponents away, creating a better situation. This is important around the opponent's goal. Teammates who move out towards the wings will remove undesirable chokes around the goal, increasing the scoring chances; this tactic could cause the opposition to make a critical defensive error.

SCORING

It is fairly common to see a player become quite upset after missing a seemingly easy goal. Scoring a goal under pressure is different from scoring in reduced pressure situations. To improve a player's scoring average, scoring must be practiced under dynamic conditions, but the conditions must be controlled. So instead of permitting the customary "place the ball on the ground and kick at the goalkeeper" warm-up before games or practices, players should have a more disciplined method of scoring practice. There are drills designed for this purpose. Chapter 6 contains the once-on-drill, the heading drill and the trap and shoot drills. These are preferred to the less practical, yet common, scoring practice mentioned above.

Young players often score a goal by pushing the ball ahead about 10' (3 meters), running up to it, and then making the kick. This method of scoring is only somewhat effective with very young players or against little defense. Players must learn to kick the ball from near or under the body to score goals in serious soccer. This is a technique that comes with disciplined drilling.

Penalty Kicks

Penalty shots are taken from 12 yards (11 meters) out in outdoor soccer, directly in front of the center of the goal. (See Law XIV on page 190 for an explanation.)

Offensive Play. Penalty kicks look easy, but under game pressure, scoring can be difficult for a player who has not had very recent practice making this type of kick.

It is advantageous for each young player desiring to take penalty kicks in games to choose only one style of kick and only one corner to aim at. In indoor soccer, the ball is best placed in an upper corner, while in outdoor soccer the ball is best placed in a lower corner, for the following reason. In both cases, the goalkeeper will have difficulty defending the aforesaid corners. Do not worry that a goalkeeper will learn a particular player's preferred corner. With so few penalty shots, this is not a problem and a well-placed shot at the chosen corner is not an easy save anyway.

The method for aiming and kicking is illlustrated in Fig. 4-7. Sight over the ball to a point inside the goal 2' (.6 meter) from the goalpost for the push pass or the basic instep kick; there should not be sufficient spin with these kicks to cause any significant curving of the trajectory. If older players pick another type of kick, they must compensate for the spin by moving the line of sight over to the right or left by approximately 1 ½ ' (.5 meter). This applies to either side of the goal.

The rear sight is a sighted point on the ball. This sighting point can be accomplished by picking a visual point on the ball, or the ball can be moved so one can use some mark on the ball. The point must be at the midpoint elevation of the ball to keep it from rising or just slightly below the midpoint to cause it to rise. Start the run of the kick from approximately 5' (1.5 meters) back directly in line with the ball and target. The eye must be kept on that spot (rear sight) at all times. With total concentration, the kick is to be made to the chosen point on the ball without ever looking up at the target. Kick straight through into the targeted direction and only look up after the ball has reached

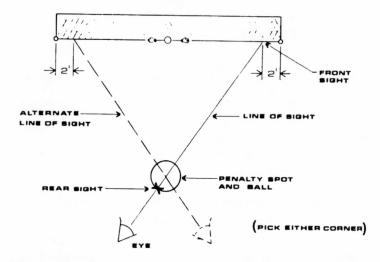

Figure 4-7. Setting up the penalty kick. In practices, carefully sight the targeted point with a point on the ball. In games, you must deceive the goalkeeper as to which corner is your chosen one.

the goal. It is important that accuracy is not sacrificed for speed. This kick does not have to travel at a high velocity. Players must practice this kick until they realize that a premeditated effort is needed to hit the target consistently. The kick should be practiced each season by the best players on the team. During games, deception is important as to which corner is the chosen one, and the player should therefore disguise his plans. Note that running directly behind the ball towards the target does not indicate which corner is the chosen one.

Defensive Play. Often, goalkeepers choose a direction (right or left) and dive towards that direction, supposedly at the time the ball is kicked. The reasoning behind this move is to give himself a $^{50}/_{50}$ chance of saving goals. It may look good, but picking the correct corner seems to be successful only about 25 percent of the time, so it may be preferable for the goalkeeper to remain stationary until he sees what direction the ball is kicked. This way, if a kick is made near the center of the goal, a save on either side can be made. On the other hand, a kicked ball with a reasonable velocity at 2' (.6 meter) or less to one of the posts probably cannot be saved anyway a goalkeeper attempts to do so. If a goal is scored, a goalkeeper may also take it personally, although he probably did not cause the infraction. If he did not cause it, he should be reassured that the goal was unsavable and he is not at fault. This way, the goalkeeper can concentrate on the game and not on himself.

Referees

Referees must be strong willed and must not be intimidated by players or spectators. When two or more players are involved in a brawl, all players involved should be shown the red card immediately. On the one hand, the referees must show that they do not stand for any nonsense, but on the other hand, they should promote a good soccer contest with as little interference as possible. They are to enforce the laws of the game but are to allow the game to flow smoothly. Now and then a referee will act like a dictator. This activity must not be permitted, and proper warnings should be given to this person by the league. There is a difference between an individual in control and one that abuses his authority. There are times when a game gets rough or the spectators are getting unruly. Then it is up to the referee to be in control and stop the game to issue the proper warnings before continuing the match. If the situation does not improve, it is advisable to discontinue the match. The league will then decide upon the outcome of the match.

Refereeing is a very important factor in this sport, but it is frequently taken for granted. Games are very often, refereed fairly, and no one takes notice of the referees. That is their job, and when it is done well, everyone concerned goes about planning for the next game. There are those times, however, when situations get out of hand that are either directly or indirectly caused by poor officiation. The situation can get so bad that parents and spectators can get into angry verbal battles. Sometimes this anger is translated into violence. Referees should be trained to handle situations when the spectators and players become troublesome, but it is preferable to train referees on avoidance of problems and situations that can lead to hostility.

If a league is serious about soccer, it will institute an ongoing referees' program. This is just as important as any other league function. The program should have a "civilian" referees' coordinator linking the chief referee with the league president. A major responsibility for this

individual is to insure that the chief referee conducts ongoing training. This ongoing training naturally covers the laws of the game along
with numerous examples of how these laws apply. This person's job is
also to oversee many of the games and follow up on reports of poor
officiation. The league president should not be allowed to treat this
position lightly.

The following is a situation that I have seen repeated many times,
and it is a precursor to an angry emotional situation. A player provokes
another player, perhaps by tripping, kicking, pulling his jersey or by
some other violent act. This same offending player then engages in
another violent act once or twice more and is not penalized by the referee. Finally, the player to whom these violent acts were directed retaliates. This same player is now the only one who is penalized. How will
this player react? Normally, he will not take this repeated attack on
himself calmly. If the referee had done his job right the first time, the
situation would most likely have remained under control. At this time,
even when in doubt about who is the guilty person, the referee should
give the yellow card or red card to both players. If the two-referee system is in effect, both referees should confer before making a decision.
Even in a three-referee system, the main referee should get the observations of the two lines-persons prior to making such decisions.

Before a game, it is a good idea for the referee to give a little talk
to the players about what he expects. When I refereed games, I liked
to say to the players: "I do the best I can to see infractions on both
sides. I may not see every infraction, but I do not favor one team over
another. I will not tolerate back-talk, swearing, or serious infractions
of the rules. I expect a clean game. Do this for me, and I promise you
a fair and enjoyable contest." I believe that I was in control of my
games and never ran into difficult situations. When a potential problem surfaced, I nipped it in the bud. I enjoyed refereeing as much as
playing and coaching the game.

Good referees in general explain infractions and often compliment players on a certain skill performed well. They may warn players for mild infractions while running alongside them. This warning
would come as a whisper that the infraction did not go unnoticed.
This action cannot help but gain respect for the referee.

Preventing situations from getting out of hand should be a top
priority for all referees. During the early minutes in a game, referees

should be alerted to rough play by one of the teams. This early roughness indicates that this behavior is condoned by the coach of that team. When players start out hacking (kicking the opponents' legs and ankles), it is an obvious sign that their coach is not acting in a responsible manner. The game should be stopped at this time and the coach reprimanded. If the rough play still continues, the game should be terminated. If the game is terminated, the referee must then make out a detailed report and submit it to the competent authority. At this time a responsible league should take notice of a coach who cannot keep her team from acting in a violent or irresponsible way. The coach's ability should be in question, no matter how much she is needed.

In order for the league to police itself and to maintain smooth game situations, it should be concerned about the quality of its players, coaches, and managers, as well as its referees. The league should require reports to be turned in by a referee when a yellow or red card is issued to a player or a caution (possibly a yellow or red card) is given to a coach or manager. These reports should explain in detail the situations that led up to the issuance of a yellow or red card. This report would go to the head referee and then to the league. There should be a punishment attached to each card or combination of cards such as a one- or two-game player suspension. Repeated incidents should cause a longer suspension. Three cautions to a coach or manager should cause a league to deal with this individual. The league should evaluate whether a coach or manager should continue in this position. If the season is nearing its end, a replacement is going to be difficult, so whether to utilize this person in the next season should be the issue of discussion.

If the above situations occur and no action is taken, the league is not acting in a responsible manner towards the majority of its players, coaches, and managers. This lack of action is shortsighted because these types of incidents indicate deepseated problems that can only worsen. Only a league that polices itself is a healthy and responsible one that can produce excellent soccer players. The referee is responsible for providing such feedback.

THE THREE- AND TWO-PERSON SYSTEMS

There are two systems of refereeing used in amateur soccer: the three-person system and the two-person system. The three-person system is comprised of the head referee and two lines-persons (usually referred to as lines-men).

With a three-person system, the head referee is solely responsible for making decisions. Line-persons are assistants of the referee. The head referee makes her own decisions on enforcement of the Laws of the Game. The head referee should consider the intervention of a lines-person however, if this head referee has not seen some particular incident brought to her attention by one of the lines-persons.

The job of the lines-person mostly consists of raising a flag when the ball crosses totally over the touch line and goal line. By observing which team last touched the ball before it went over the goal line, she then indicates whether the next play is a corner kick or a goal kick. The lines-person is also to signal when a player is in an offside position. The decision whether to call a player offside is solely the responsibility of the head referee, however.

In house leagues, it is customary to have a volunteer lines-person appointed by each team. Generally, their job is limited to signaling when the ball totally crosses the touch line and also indicating which team is awarded the throw-in.

A two-person system is used only in amateur soccer. With a two-person system, there are only two referees and no lines-people. Generally, each referee covers only one-half of the field and both referees have equal responsibility for overseeing the game. In the second half of the game, it is important that the referees remain on their same side of the field. This way, each referee will be covering the opposite team when the teams change direction. This helps neutralize any bias that may occur towards either team.

There are certain advantages to both refereeing systems. First there is a matter of economics that can be generally balanced with the level of play. If the level of play is high, the three-person system is usually chosen. In house leagues, the desire for keeping the fees as low as possible dictates the use of a single referee with volunteer lines-persons. In other amateur leagues, the two-person refereeing system is usually less costly than the three-person system. This would be the main reason for preferring the two-person system.

There is another consideration that is worth discussion. In amateur soccer the level of refereeing can range from very poor to excellent. For the young age house-league games, the leagues generally draft as referees players who are just a few years older than the players in the game. Some of these youthful referees have very little training and knowledge of the laws. (See Appendix on page 179, "Laws of the Game.") These referees can be out on a field doing little more then blowing the whistle at start times. They can also cause the wrong team to be the winner by biased officiation or just by having complete lack of control of the game. This system of refereeing, when not overseen by a referees' coordinator, can have serious negative consequences for the development of young soccer players. Also, better quality refereeing will generally not occur if refereeing is not controlled by the league paying for these services.

The two-person refereeing system has certain advantages. If a young inexperienced referee is paired with an experienced and unbiased older referee, the younger referee can get some excellent on-the-job training, especially if little training is available to her otherwise. When a serious infraction occurs, both referees can discuss the foul and any punitive action for the offense; thus reduced bias is built into this system. In addition, one referee may not see as much as two referees, each of whom generally has only one-half of the field to cover. This can permit a better observation of possible infringements that may occur anywhere on the field.

PREPARATION FOR GAMES

Referees are at their best if they are prepared for each game. Referees, like everyone else, make mistakes. Embarrassing mistakes can happen when a referee forgets which team kicked off the ball at the start of a game, which direction the kick-off was, what time the half started, who scored, what the score is. It may seem that there should be no difficulty remembering all of the above, but when one is concentrating on the game, one is bound to forget a detail now and then. This can all be remedied if the referee develops certain self-disciplined habits. The referee should have a check list to follow before the start of each game. The list includes a red and yellow card, a whistle, a watch, a piece of paper and a pencil, and a reminder to take the game ball at halftime. A short before-game speech for the players may also be included. The list, cards, and the pencil and papers can be tucked into the sock.

THE OFFSIDE LAW

Everyone involved is soccer should understand the offside law. Many people think it is complicated, but it isn't. The details of this law are as follows:

The offside law only has an effect on players when they are in their opponent's half of the field.

If an attacking player who doesn't have the ball is ahead of it, this player is offside if there is just one opponent ahead of him. Note that an opponent is any opposing player, including the goalkeeper.

This player is not offside if he is on line with a second opponent.

A player is not offside if he runs to a normally offside position after the ball has been kicked.

A player can never be offside if he receives a ball directly from a corner kick, goal kick, or a throw-in.

A player in an offside position is not to be penalized for it unless he is there to seek an advantage.

The penalty for offside infraction is an indirect free-kick.

There are times when a referee incorrectly calls an offside infraction of Law XI. If a player is offside, he shall be penalized for being there only if he is seeking to have an advantage over the other team by taking part in a play, by attempting to get the ball, or by screening an opponent. If a player passes the ball to the left side, but a player is offside on the right side, there is no advantage to being offside and there is no infringement of Law XI. If a pass is made in the vicinity of an offside player, however, the play should be stopped and the other team awarded an indirect free-kick.

Referees should be individually tested for this aspect of the rule. Calling offside for any person in the offside position or on line with the ball is incorrect. When done repeatedly, it can frustrate and anger even the most level-headed person.

COACHES' EVALUATION OF REFEREES

This subject is usually not taken seriously by leagues. Leagues seem to resist evaluating referees, and yet one will often hear many verbal complaints about officiation, especially about certain poor referees. Many people just hope that the next game will have good refereeing and don't bother to lodge an official complaint about the present poorly officiated game. Since the league pays for the services of the referees, however, it should exercise some control over it. Most of the games that are played will have satisfactory refereeing, but there are times when this will not occur. A league should strive for 100 percent satisfactory refereeing.

Excellent refereeing nearly 100 percent of the time can be achieved if a simple common sense evaluation is applied to this aspect of the game. The common sense approach is not to have each referee evaluated after each game. Coaches will just not comply with this type of directive, especially if their team was victorious, but they will probably fill out a form if they lost or seemed to have lost the game based upon poor officiation. It is thus through the losing coaches that facts about a particular poor referee may surface.

This is how an evaluation system can work. Each coach should be given enough forms at the beginning of each season to cover all games. During playoffs, they should receive another set. Before the start whistle, each referee is to sign each coach's form and print her name. After the game, each coach either discards or fills out the form and sends it to the referees' coordinator or league president. The disposition of the form is up to the coach or manager of each team. The league can then use common sense to evaluate those forms that report a particular referee. If a referee has been reported three times, it is time for a committee to review this person's record. If a pattern is observed via the submitted forms, the committee should either retrain the referee before she is given another assignment, suspend her, or oversee her next game. A suggested referees review form is illustrated below.

A referee coordinator position may not seem to be important to a league that has always been without this position, but a league that is serious about producing top quality players will give this matter some serious thought. Fair and knowledgeable refereeing is an important component in the development of players who take the game seriously. If the league does not consider top quality officiation important, the players will also have the same attitude.

There is one other point worth considering: giving referees higher pay, especially in the lower ranks. This will make the job more attractive and competitive. It is important to remember that getting more experienced and better trained referees will cause you fewer problems and help reduce the violence on the field. In addition, when the pay is low, your league may find some referees do not show up for games.

<u>SUGGESTED REFEREE REVIEW FORM</u>

DATE OF GAME: _____

REFEREES SIGNATURES (OBTAIN SIGNATURES BEFORE GAME):

1. _____ / PRINT _____

2. _____ / PRINT _____

3. _____ / PRINT _____

1. Did you win or lose?
   Win____ Lose____

2. Did the referees call pushing or kicking fouls?
   Yes___ No___ Some___

3. Did the referees have control of the game if it seemed excessively rough?
   Yes___No___

4. a. Were yellow cards given out or should they have been given out? _____

   b. Should a red card have been given out? _____

   c. If your team received yellow or red cards, were there any previous cir-
      cumstances that could have caused this incident? ____
      Explain on the back of this form.

5. Did the referees encourage and teach good soccer practices?
   Yes___No___Not Sure___

6. Write in ratings of good, fair, or poor:
   Referee #1_____ #2_____ #3_____.

7. For any additional comments, use the back of this form.

League: Under 8__ 10__ 12__ 14__ 16__ 19__ (check one)

Your team: _____

Opposing team: _____

Field of play: _____

Signature of coach _____ / PRINT _____

Mail to:

5. Goalkeeping

The goalkeeper can make the difference between a winning or a losing team. The defense of the goal is just one aspect of an experienced goalkeeper's job. While a goalkeeper must have technical competence, the extra winning difference comes from defense management. This person should make it a practice to rule over her defense people; as indicated previously, the goalkeeper must eventually control the total defense to protect the goal more completely. Since this player is the last person on defense and often the first person on offense, she must be conditioned to make proper decisions in regards to the defensive players for defending as well as attacking. It is advisable that she also learns to play out in the field, to understand the field player's pressures as well as to develop some field experience for those occasions when she must leave the 18-yard (16.5-meter) goal area. Beyond the goal area, her hands are disabled for use, so she should also attain other nongoalkeeping soccer skills.

The goalkeeper should constantly be assessing the field to determine whether midfield gaps become frequent and to alert the players when this is occurring. This player has basically three defensive roles to fulfill; the third role listed below includes an attack element. Early in one's goalkeeping career, however, generally only role 1 below will apply.

1. To guard the goal; this is the third echelon of defense.
2. To control her backfield players; this is the second echelon of defense.
3. To watch for midfield gaps and to start attacks by utilizing rearward open players. Adequate midfield defensive coverage helps to reduce

the pressure in your defensive zone, and your midfielders' offensive ball control also reduces this pressure. Both of these aspects are the goalkeeper's first echelon of defense.

Note that each higher-level echelon protects each lower echelon. The goalkeeper's lines or echelons of defense are repeatedly emphasized throughout the book to insure that the coach, goalkeeper, and other players thoroughly understand the importance of defense for winning games and championships.

When young players begin their goalkeeping career, they should be instructed that catching the ball is not the only way to make a save. Punching and deflecting balls that are difficult to catch into a safe area is just as important as making caught-ball saves. The goalkeeper will inevitably catch more balls as she gains experience, and eventually, there will be fewer opponent goals scored as the goalkeeper begins directing the defensive teammates. While it is the job of each defense person to know how to defend correctly, it is readily observed that they make mistakes in judgment, so the goalkeeper should learn early in her career to watch her defenders. But until this occurs, you, the coach, must do this job (as long as coaching from the sidelines is permissible).

As mentioned, catching the ball is not the most important save that can be made. Punching the ball wide towards the wings is more important for a young player. Goalkeepers should adopt the policy, "When in doubt punch or push it out." This also means to deflect the ball over the goalpost using the fingertips. The correct action depends on several situation factors that come naturally with experience. Whichever action is taken, however, the ball should not be deflected into the center of the field or to a side of the field where an opponent is lurking unmarked.

Coaches must relentlessly remind the goalkeeper to call out when she wants to receive, push-out, or punch the ball. This player must verbally express in an authoritative manner, "keeper," "goalie," "goalkeeper," or something similar. This is virtually the only loud command by a player that is permitted in soccer. Expressions such as "I've got it" and "mine" are not permitted by any player at any time. This type of expression would be penalized by an indirect kick for the opposition.

When the goalkeeper has definite possession of the ball, an opposing player cannot kick it out of her hands or chase after the goalie while she is attempting to kick or throw the ball. The goalie can take up to four steps with the ball; then, she can throw it, kick it, or dribble it. The ball cannot be picked up again once it is placed on the ground. Special rules for indoor soccer may specify that the ball cannot be passed back to the goalkeeper.

The young goalkeeper usually starts her career with several disadvantages: coaches normally do not spend much time training the goalkeeper, so goalkeepers usually participate in training drills with the rest of the team. In fact, some get no special training at all and must acquire the knowledge by themselves. This is a disservice to the goalkeeper and the team.

Naturally, it is preferable that each team have a coach who spends time training the goalkeeper while the field players' training exercises are in progress. If a person with goalkeeper's knowledge can be obtained, even if only for a few practice sessions, this would be ideal. If no such person is available, however, a person with little or no soccer knowledge can be utilized. In either case, the trainer will need direction from you, the coach. If a person has soccer experience, he will probably want to kick balls at the training goalkeeper from all directions, but this is not the proper method to train a goalkeeper. You should know how to give this assistant proper instruction rather than passing on the responsibility to him. The following guidelines should be followed, with emphasis that catching the ball need only be a minor part of making saves for the novice goalkeeper.

The trainer should not kick the ball at the goalkeeper, at least most of the time. Throwing the ball is much more efficient because repeated accuracy is needed to get the ball exactly where a particular type of save must be practiced. Kicking some ground balls can be permitted only to break the monotony for the trainer, but it is the goalkeeper who needs the practice, not the trainer. This should be thoroughly understood by the trainer.

The goalkeeper must be reminded to stand about 5' (1 ½ meters) out from the goal line, and she should always be balancing the angle (explained later) on either side of the goal. The balls should be thrown to the corners, both high and low, over the goalkeeper's head. The trainer should also throw spinning bouncers. The spinning bouncers are thrown with both hands in a spinning motion. Spin the ball between the hands before it gets released (thrown). The throws (the shots on goal) should be made fast and slow but with many repetitions of the same type. The trainer should observe the training player's concentration during activities of catching, pushing, and throwing the ball back to himself. Sloppy ball returns to the trainer indicate that the novice player is not paying attention to her own activities. Also, assure that all caught balls are habitually brought into the stomach or the chest, even with the easy saves. If the trainer is properly guided, you should have good results from the trained goalkeeper(s) during games.

The goalkeeper is taught to develop the ability to win games based upon control of the defense. Since you will not see this happen at the younger level, however, you should have a defense coach help your goalkeeper during games (if it is permitted in your league). The defense coach should concentrate only on the goalkeeper's defense and offense to teach the goalkeeper defensive strategy for full goal protection at all times. This should also give your team the edge in close matches. With a good defense in place, the goalkeeper should be making infrequent "spectacular" saves because she is correctly positioning herself, thus making nearly all saves look easy.

Goalie's Stance

The goalkeeper's stance is as follows: the feet are positioned to be less than a ball's width apart to insure that the ball cannot pass through the legs. This player is to be standing on his toes and leaning slightly forward. The arms are to be outstretched for balance and defense. The face should indicate a confident individual, and this person should "want the ball." With this stance, the player is in an optimum position to spring into action. (See Fig. 5-2.)

Catching in the Air

Balls kicked or headed at or nearly at a novice goalkeeper can be obviously caught. Whenever possible, this player should adjust his

Figure 5-1. The correct protection of the ball after it has been caught. Note the elevated knee that is brought up at that moment.

position prior to catching the ball by getting directly behind it. Catching the ball off to the side imposes certain risks because it can slip through the hands without the benefit of the body as a backstop. After the ball is caught, it must be brought into the midsection or chest. The arms and hands should wrap around the ball to hold onto it as if for dear life. This must be done at all times, even during the most simple catches. It must be instilled into the novice goalkeeper that the ball is not secured when it is in the hands, but only when it is protected by the hands, arms, and midsection or chest (the midsection is the best place).

It must be noted that whenever the goalkeeper is in the air, he is vulnerable to getting hit by an opponent. Goalkeepers use a bit of protection against "accidental collisions" by bringing one knee up to about the midsection level until any danger of collision has ended. This is illustrated in Fig. 5-1.

Positioning

The goalkeeper should normally stand about 4' to 5' (1.2 to 1.5 meters) in front of the goal line. This enables him to be safely away

Figure 5-2. The goalkeeper's stance. The legs are nearly closed to prevent the ball from passing through them.

from the goal when catching a fast ball. If the ball is fully over the goal line, inside the goalposts, it is a goal even if the goalkeeper is holding it with his feet inside of the field. Another reason for this player being positioned "out" is to reduce the angles on either side of him from an attacker's shot on goal. Fig. 5-3 shows the balanced angle coverage on both sides of the goal. The further out the goalkeeper is, the smaller the target angles become for the attacker. Naturally, the distance "out" is offset by the attacker's scoring possibilities: the attacker could chip the ball over the goalkeeper's head, she could dribble around the goalkeeper, or she could pass the ball to a near nonoffside teammate.

When an attacking player has a break-away, the goalkeeper's best chance of preventing a goal is to come out and meet the attacker. The timing is important. First the goalkeeper should remain in position and estimate the attacker's speed. Then charge this attacking player and meet her at about 12 yards (11 meters) out. Another choice is to position himself by balancing the angles on both sides of the goal at approximately a 12' (3 ½ meters) radius from the center point under the goal. For example, if the attacker is coming directly down the center of the field, then the goalkeeper should be approximately 12' (3 ½ meters) directly in front of the goal. Or if the attacker is coming at an oblique angle, the goalkeeper is to position himself at the point on the

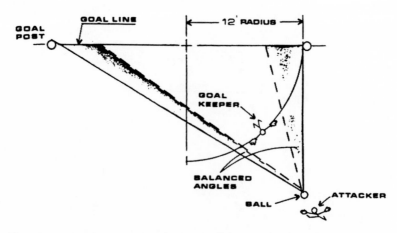

Figure 5-3. The figure shows the goalkeeper remaining stationary during a breakaway by an opposing player. The goalkeeper must always balance the angles on either side. In this instance, coming out more than 5' reduces the target area for the attacker.

arc of the imaginary 12' (3 ½ meters) radius shown in Fig. 5-3. This player must be constantly balancing the angles on both sides of the goal. (Under normal defensive conditions, the goalkeeper would be only about 5' [1 ½ meters] out, but still balancing the angles.)

It is extremely important for the goalkeeper to make a decision and not waver or change his plan. Whether the decision is to go out and meet the opponent or to make a stand, there should be no hesitation. If the attacker senses any hesitation on the part of the goalkeeper, she will probably score. When the goalkeeper is confident, the opponent will often kick directly at him or to a point for an easy save.

For corner kicks, the young novice goalkeeper should stand on the goal line, about ⅓ of the way from the far goalpost. If the goalkeeper is too close to the near post, he may not be able to recover in time to make a save if the shot goes to the rear post. (See Fig. 5-4-A.) The triangles represent the defenders.

At the more advanced levels of soccer, the goalkeeper should stand out about ½ to ⅓ of the way from the near post. She should then set up a defense as shown in Fig. 5-4-B. This defensive measure prevents goals from being scored by ground-ball corner kicks in front of the goal.

It should be noted that the defensive strategy shown in Fig. 5-4-B

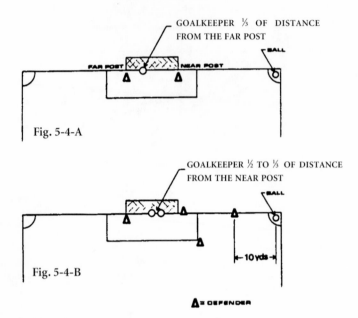

Figure 5-4. Defensive setup against a corner kick. Fig. 5-4-A is for the novice goalkeeper, while Fig. 5-4-B is for the advanced goalkeeper.

is different at higher levels of soccer compared to lower-level soccer because the advanced strategy will tend to confuse younger players. It is simpler just to teach young field players to place one player at the far post and another player at the near post.

After the ball is caught, it must be speedily brought back into play. When the goalkeeper learns to be observant, she will be taking notice of player positions at all times. This is an obvious advantage for the goalkeeper when observing her teammates' positions prior to making a potential save. This advantage can obviate searching for an open teammate in order to get the ball quickly into play.

Punching

Punching the ball out into a safe area is an effective way to make a difficult save. It is a very efficient defense against corner kicks where the ball is thrust into the air space in front of a crowded goal. The method of punching the ball is to place the fists together and punch as

Figure 5-5. Punching the ball out safely. The fists are together, and the knuckles are flat. Tuck the thumb in just as in a boxing punch.

if the right and left hands were glued to each other; tuck the thumbs back to protect them against injury during punching. Sometimes one fist will be used when the ball cannot be reached by both fists. Coaches should constantly be reminding young goalkeepers, "When in doubt punch or push it out."

The punching technique is practiced by an assistant throwing the ball to the corners or over the goalkeeper's head to a point where catching it safely is uncertain. The goalkeeper should punch the ball to the wing area, high and far out. This way it is not likely to be settled and controlled by an opponent for another quick shot at the goal. (See Fig. 5.5 for the correct method of punching the ball.)

Tipping

Tipping the ball is a deflection technique. When a ball is not safely in the range of a sure catch, this technique is used to alter the path of the ball. Tipping the ball outside of the vertical or horizontal goalpost is done with the fingertips and not with the whole hand. This is impor-

Figure 5-6. Tipping the ball over the net. The fingertips, not the fingers or hands, are used to alter the flight of the ball. The speed of the ball must not slow down.

tant to understand because it is desired to alter only the ball's path, not its speed. Altering the ball's speed can produce a goal because the ball may be deflected over the goalkeeper's hands and slowed down sufficiently to pass under the horizontal goalpost. This can occur if the whole hand or hands absorb some of the ball's momentum.

This technique is best practiced in an actual goal and preferably one with a net. For the horizontal-crossbar deflection technique, the ball should be thrown over the head of the goalkeeper in order that he must jump up at it to deflect it over the goalpost. (See Fig. 5-6.) For the vertical-goalpost deflection technique, the same throwing method applies but the player must lunge sideways to deflect the ball. Note it is instructive to make several throws towards the crossbar and permit the goalkeeper to actually slow the ball down with the palms of the hands in such a way that the ball does not go over the goalpost but instead goes into the net.

Catching Low Balls and Direct Balls

From the goalie's stance, the goalkeeper gets directly behind the ball and brings the legs together, bending over as shown in Fig. 5-7.

Figure 5-7. Catching low balls. The legs must be closed sufficiently to prevent the ball from passing through them.

After catching the ball, he must bring it into the midsection or chest. Do not allow the goalkeeper to assume it is an easy save even if it is a slow roller. The techniques described in "Catching the Ball from the Air" are not to be deviated from at any time.

Lunging

Goalkeepers must learn to lunge to their right or left to make saves. Lunging for the ball is not very difficult to teach young players if they are permitted to acquire the confidence needed for this endeavor slowly. The following is a very good practice exercise to help build this confidence.

In a soft grassy area cleared of any hard objects, the player should lunge onto the ball completely from the air. Prior to landing, he must grab the ball with the hands as shown in Fig. 5-8. Note that for this exercise, the ball is placed at a special distance away from the player that is measured as follows: The player is to lay face down on the grass with outstretched arms. Then the ball is placed at his fingertips. Next allow the player to stand without moving the position of his feet. Now, with the player facing and leaning toward the ball, he should lunge at the ball and contact it with the palms of both hands before his body touches the ground. If the player is apprehensive, move the ball closer until he is comfortable with this position. Note that the body should

Figure 5-8. When lunging, the goalkeeper should grab the ball with both hands before his body touches the ground.

not touch the ground until the hands have first contacted the ball. The ball will cushion the impact. After landing, the player must keep his eyes on the ball while curling the body up into a ball to protect the soccer ball. The player will have both arms and knees securely wrapped around the ball, pressing it into the midsection. This exercise should be repeated many times, gradually moving the ball out to the original measured position if it was moved closer, until the player develops confidence in diving and securing the ball. When this confidence has been developed, make artificial goalposts by using field markers, soccer balls, or clothing by placing them in a soft, grassy, cleared area 18' (5 ½ meters) to 24' (7.32 meters) wide. With the training goalkeeper in the goalie's stance, roll the ball into the corners of the "goalposts" and have the goalkeeper dive at the ball as explained earlier. At first, roll the ball slowly and make sure that the player actually dives in the same manner as when using the stationary ball. As confidence develops, roll the ball faster. The method described here helps reduce the player's fear of diving. Advanced goalkeepers may dive differently. The coach and the player may desire to investigate these diving techniques from other authoritative sources. Note that the coach should experiment with the above technique herself before deciding to give instructions to novice players.

Punting

Young goalkeepers punt the ball nearly every time they take possession of it. As the field players mature and can maintain ball possession with strong shielding and trapping skills, punting should not

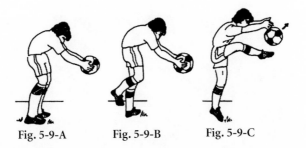

Fig. 5-9-A   Fig. 5-9-B   Fig. 5-9-C

Figure 5-9. The initial positions for the punt and the final punt.

be the goalkeeper's first choice. Nevertheless, punting must be learned. The novice goalkeeper should punt the ball repeatedly until she develops confidence and the ability to get the ball sufficiently up-field. This training might include twenty minutes during each practice when the player and the trainer punt the ball back and forth to each other. Repetition is important. The training is more efficient when several balls are utilized and the player is permitted to make repetitive kicks.

The method of punting for a right-footed kicker is as follows (reverse the body sides for a left-footed kicker): Extend the ball out in front of the right foot at about 12"(30 cm). The head, neck, back, and legs should look something like a question mark when viewing the profile of the body. The ball is held at groin level on the right side of the body. The left foot should be slightly forward and both knees slightly bent. (See Fig. 5-9-A.) The next step is to bring the right knee up nearly parallel to the ground as shown in Fig. 5-9-B and drop the ball. The right foot should contact the ball at the bony part of the instep after being dropped only a few inches (about 15 cm) as shown in Fig. 5-9-C. Note the kick is from the knee and the leg that kicked the ball is following through the kick. These final kicking steps are vital for ball kicking; the player must keep her eyes on the ball during contact (and the head in the same place after the ball and the foot make contact) and must follow through. Photo 3 shows the final stages of a punt.

Goal Kicking

Goal kicks are taken by your team when the opposition was the last to touch the ball before it went over the goal line. The ball is placed

Photo 3. The final stages of the full-body-coordinated punt. Note the correct-
ness of the head position of the kicker, who has not prematurely looked up to
observe the ball's flight.

in the goal area on the same side where it went out of play. It is usually
placed on the line, but it can be kicked from anywhere in that half of
the goal area.

It is advisable for the goalkeeper to take all goal kicks. As mentioned before, having another player take them while the goalkeeper
stands by leaves nine potential receivers to eleven opponent potential
receivers on the field. The odds are even worse when an undisciplined
team leaves two or three others just hanging back as nonpotential
receivers.

It is to the team's advantage to get the ball into play as soon as
possible, not giving the opponents sufficient time to mark its players.
If a defender is unmarked, the goalkeeper may pass him the ball. If
this same player is then pressured, the goalkeeper may ask for the ball
back. If the ball is returned to the goalkeeper, your team will have lost
its attack advantage and the goalkeeper must then kick the ball up-
field.

The goal kick is usually made with the instep kick following the
rules for kicking outlined in Chapter 3. To get the power for obtaining distance, the whole body must be coordinated with the kick. Photo
4 shows a player making a goal kick. Note the goalkeeper in the final
stages of this kick in Photo 4 is following through and has his head

Photo 4. The goal kick is photographed just as the ball has been propelled by the right foot. This photo also shows that the kicker's head has remained down, thus illustrating that the eyes must remain fixed on the ball during the kick.

down (is not up looking at the target) with his eyes on the ball. Note also that the whole body participates in the kicking procedure.

Propelling the Ball by Hand

Throwing the ball to teammates is the preferred passing method for ball control soccer. These throwing methods are:

THE UNDERHANDED THROW

The ball can be rolled to the feet of a teammate in the same manner as throwing a bowling ball, with the nonthrowing hand holding the ball prior to its release.

THE OVERHAND THROW

Throwing the ball overhand is accomplished in the same manner as throwing an oblong football. It should be thrown to the receiver's feet in order for this person to control it easily. It is not desirable to throw a high ball or a bouncer. These passes take several seconds to settle and could cause an interception of the ball.

THE OVERHANDED TWO-HANDED THROW

Throwing the ball with two hands over one's head is accomplished in the same fashion as a soccer throw-in. This two-handed throw is usually reserved for getting the ball to a teammate who is in open space. The pass is usually thrown over the head of an opponent who is between the goalkeeper and the potential receiver.

Defending Against Two Players on a Breakaway

Visualize two players of the opposing team breaking past your defensive players. This places the goalkeeper in a difficult situation. He has lost control of the defensive line and must now deal with two simultaneous attackers. A good defensive strategy is as follows: The goalkeeper moves to a point about five feet directly in front of the goal to position himself between the attacker with the ball and the goal (the same situation as described in "Positioning" above). The goalkeeper now concentrates and defends against only this player. If the ball is passed, at that instant the goalkeeper repositions himself in front of the second player and now maintains total concentration on this second opponent. At this time, he should does not let himself be distracted by the previous player.

An exercise that simulates the above situation can be practiced with the whole team by forming two lines behind the halfline. The first player from each line starts the attack (one with the ball and the other without the ball). As the attackers approach the goal, the goalkeeper concentrates on the player with the ball. This player may take a shot on goal or may pass the ball to her teammate. The attack must be made with the intention of beating the goalkeeper. After the shot on goal has been taken, the player who has taken the shot retrieves the ball and both players then go to the rear of the opposite line.

6. Drills

Homework

Coaches and parents should continuously encourage homework drills. This section covers drills to be done by the individual player on her own time inside or outside the house. Some drills are to be performed against a flat wall such as a solid building wall without windows. For each player to get the maximum benefit from soccer training, she must own a soccer ball. This ball should not be a rubber ball or the lowest price vinyl type. These balls are painful when headed and do not have a correct bounce.

TRAPPING AND KICKING

The surest method for learning how to trap a ball stationary at one's feet is to repeatedly kick and trap a ball against a wall or stairs or to throw the ball against a ball rebound board described in Part III of this chapter. Walls or stairs must be constructed of solid wood, concrete, or other hard, nonbrittle components.

Caution is strongly advised: walls and stairs used in this drill must not be constructed of plaster or thin paneling. There must not be any fragile objects around the wall or stairs such as a light fixture, a smoke detector, a window, or any other breakable object. If a basement wall or stairway is used, protect appliances, windows, or anything else that can be broken by the ball's impact. Walls and stairs of any type should not be used without the owner's permission. The ceiling must be high enough to prevent head, hand, or arm injury when jumping.

Hard walls, on the one hand, rebound the soccer ball nearly as fast as the initial kick velocity and return it with a predictable angle and speed. Stairs, on the other hand, return the ball at unpredictable angles and speeds. This unpredictability gives good practice because the player must be able to trap the ball with his head, chest, body, thighs, calves, or feet. In any case, the kicking must be hard enough to get the amount of ball velocity that could be expected in actual game situations. During the trapping drill, speed, accuracy, balance, and coordination will be developed if self-discipline is applied. The player must make the kick, go to the ball if it is far from the wall, trap the ball dead at his feet, make one slight play on the ball to set it up for the next kick, and then kick it again. Traps and kicks are performed with both sides of the body. While kicking and trapping, the player is to follow each step as discussed in the particular skill sections in Chapter 3 — "Basic Trapping," "Basic Instep Kick," etc.

The following should be avoided:

1. Soft kicking
2. Kicking most of the balls back at first contact instead of trapping them dead at the feet
3. Very hard kicking
4. Sloppy trapping

Volleying

This practice is extremely important if a player wishes to use a volley accurately and effectively in games. It is performed in a soccer field by throwing the ball in the air, letting it bounce, and then volleying the ball to a partner following the rules described in Part I, Chapter 9. Always remember to follow Rule 1 for kicking (keep the eyes on the ball at all times during and immediately after the kick).

Dribbling

Along with trapping, dribbling is a skill whose level must be constantly upgraded. Unless these two skills are second nature to a soccer player, she will soon become obsolete. The following dribbling drills should be part of a routine for every level of soccer player just as serious musicians must practice scales.

Fig. 6-1-A   Fig. 6-1-B

Figure. 6-1. The sensitivity of touch drill. Fig. 6-1-A, shows the pattern of using the inside and outside of the foot. Fig. 6-1-B shows the 180-degree turn.

Dribble and Run. The player is to run with the ball and dribble it as close to his feet as possible. Every step should touch the ball while altering the touch with both feet. At times, just one foot is used and the ball should still be pushed with every step, that is, with the right or left foot. The run should be about the distance of a full field and back. Note that the ball is pushed, not tapped. The slightest push controls the ball; a tap does not control it. The eyes should be used to observe the surroundings, not the ball.

Sensitivity of Touch. This drill can be performed indoors or outdoors, provided that the area is clean, free of debris, and not slippery. The shoes and socks may be removed. The player dribbles the ball around while running on the toes in a ten-feet (3 meters) long figure eight. (See Fig. 6-1.) With every step, the player touches the ball using the inside and outside of the foot. Turns 180 degrees in direction must be mastered. These turns are made by reaching with the foot and hooking it around in front of the ball to make it change to a direction exactly opposite to its original one. The player should stretch her arms out for balance (as a tight rope walker does). The speed of this drill will increase with practice as the player learns to turn, develops a greater sensitivity of touch, and improves her sense of balance. It should be done three to four times per week. Note that this exercise is fatiguing when done rapidly.

Jump and Ball Bounce. This drill is useful for developing balance and coordination for dribbling and is performed as follows, using the ball-contact points marked "X" in Fig. 6-2: With the ball between the feet, alternately push it back and forth near the big toes (where the toes

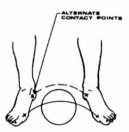

Figure 6-2. The contact points on the feet for the jump and ball-bounce drill.

meet the feet). Push the ball from one foot to the other while jump-ing up a few inches. The feet should not be flat in this exercise, but should stand on the toes. The ball should rise a few inches after each contact. There is an alternate spot back a few inches that can be used. The more rearward spot allows the dribbler more shielding protection for the ball. This exercise, if sustained for a few minutes a few times per week, will develop sensitivity and balance.

Rolling Ball. This drill is designed to give a sensitive feel for the ball. It is especially useful for ball control when playing indoor soc-cer. Standing in front of the ball, place either foot on top of the ball and roll it in a figure eight. While the player is doing this, all parts of the bottom of the front of his foot will contact the ball as it rolls beneath it. Alternate this exercise with each foot for a total of five minutes. (See Fig. 6-3.) Note that if any of these drills are given as an assignments to the players, it is a good exercise to have each drill demonstrated by the team for about 30 seconds at the start of each practice. In game play, the skills and balance developed from these drills should be readily observable.

Figure 6-3. The rolling ball drill is designed to increase the sensitivity of touch. It is best performed barefooted on a clean floor.

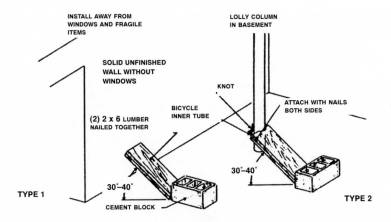

Figure 6-4. The specifications for the ball rebound board. This device is used to rebound thrown balls for trapping and heading. The practice must be carried out in accordance with the skills and cautions outlined in this book.

PRACTICING WITH THE BALL REBOUND BOARD

The ball rebound board is a simple device used to practice trapping and heading of balls that arrive at the player in the air. The angle of the ball coming to the player can be adjusted by changing the rebound angle by a few degrees. (See Fig. 6-4 for its fabrication and setup.) It can easily be constructed of 2" × 6" (6 cm × 15 cm) lumber and easily set up. The block illustrated is constructed of concrete; it is not its lighter counterpart called a cinder block. The ball rebound board must not be used near fragile objects such as doors, windows, light fixtures, or smoke detectors, nor should it be placed against finished or plaster-type walls. The ceiling must be sufficiently high to allow the thrower ample clearance for throwing the ball and for preventing hand, arm, or head injury. If a light fixture is nearby, it must be well protected.

To practice all air-ball traps and heading, the ball is thrown overhand at about the center of the rebound board. It rebounds and arrives at the player in the air and is used for self-practice for any of the various traps or headers that need to be practiced. For immediate use, stand back from the rebound board by about 5' (1½ meters) and throw the ball at it. As proficiency improves, move back to about 10' (3 meters) to receive longer "passes." Practices should be about 30 repetitions about three times a week for any applicable skill that needs improving. Eventually the skills should become a reflex action.

At Practice

The question is often asked, "What are the best soccer drills for field players?" The answer comes from a simple combination of these common sense ideas: Drills should duplicate actual game situations, that is, they should come as close to actual game encounters as possible. They should teach a basic skill, or they should combine several learned skills that can be applied in pressure situations. They should hold the player's interest. They should be repeated several times throughout the season and in future years. The constant instruction of new drills is to be discouraged; reiteration of the most commonly used skills is a better training approach.

The basic skills of each player should not be assumed to be in place. These basics are trapping the ball dead at the player's feet, shielding, dribbling the ball close to the feet, accurate push passes to close open players, defensive backing up with an opponent, and moving into open spaces while dribbling. Far too often, older North American players tend to disregard basic skills for the more urgent need in games to press forward because some coaches do not consider basic skills as valuable as playing very aggressively.

KEEPING THE PLAYERS' ATTENTION

Keeping players attentive at any age is difficult, and with very young players, this is quite a task. Whenever possible, design drills as a game. Placing players in two or four lines for competition for dribbling, shooting, shoulder charging, or anything else gets them actively involved and helps to keep their attention. Getting players involved in a demonstration, especially the outspoken players, also gets their attention. There will be times, however, when it seems impossible to get any order on the training field. When players are very young, a good technique is to promise a water break when order is restored or if the drill is practiced correctly. For a coach of young players to maintain her composure, it is necessary to be creative.

Players who are disruptive must be disciplined. Naturally, the discipline must not be severe, but a coach cannot allow one or two players to interfere with the practices. These players should be given extra laps to run around the field. If a player remains a problem, then discuss the situation with the other coach or team manager and then the league. It may be necessary to contact the parent or guardian with a warning that the child will be dropped from the team if improvement in behavior is not immediate.

The coach is then faced with two apparent choices: the disruptive player remains on the team with no disciplinary action or the player is dropped from the team. If all disruptive incidents are ignored, the situation will surely worsen. The coach should be aware that if a player is dropped from the team, there will generally not be another skilled replacement player available. An intermediate solution can perhaps provide the correct answer to the problem.

TRAPPING DRILLS

Prior to the running of trapping drills, the coach must totally familiarize the players with the techniques of dribbling, basic trapping, chest traps, and the body trap described in Chapter 3.

Basic Trapping. Refer to Fig. 6-5. This drill teaches more than trapping; it also teaches the player to observe the playing field while dribbling instead of watching the ball. The figure shows two players in this drill: there are four in the next drill. Ideally, this drill is to make the players aware that they are in a simulated game condition. Use two demonstration players before beginning the drill and give an adequate explanation to help players understand why this drill is useful. For the drill, have the players mark off two imaginary lines for each set of two players, using two field markers each. The lines should be parallel and about 20' (6 meters) apart. Each participant is restricted to move only along the direction of his line.

The two players (player 1 and player 2) should both remain on the line, moving only about 10' (3 meters) in either direction along it, and they should face each other. Each player is in a simulated position of attack towards his opponent's goal in the direction that he is facing. The two players are on "opposing" teams for the moment because they each face a different goal. They will, however, be on the same team during a part of the drill sequence when it is time to pass the ball from player 1 to player 2 and vice versa.

The drill starts off when player 1 passes the ball to player 2, on the ground and quite swiftly. Player 2 goes to the ball and traps it dead at

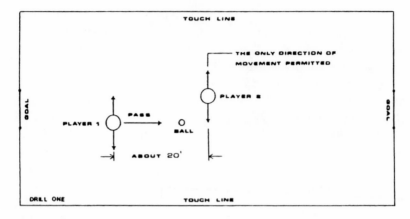

Figure 6-5. The basic trapping drill. In this drill, the players are constantly moving but are constrained to move only in the direction of the touch lines, except when adjusting their distance to maintain a constant 20' (6 meters).

his feet. At this moment, player 2 looks around, not at the ball, and begins to dribble the ball back along the line while then remaining on it at all times (the only time that the player is allowed off the line is when he is going for the ball). The dribbling consists of using each step to touch the ball with either the inside or outside of the foot. While player 2 is dribbling, he is looking around the field for an opportunity for passing the ball to player 1 (now his teammate). Each player is to make about ten touches on the ball while on the line (dribbling in one direction, then reversing direction) before passing it off. While the player with the ball is dribbling back and forth along his line, the player without the ball is also moving back and forth along his line as if anticipating a pass from a teammate in an game situation.

Young players should only make a push pass to each other, but more experienced players may use any type of kick.

Trapping and Shielding. This advanced drill is identical to Drill 1, with one exception: third and forth players are added. These players are always on the opposite team of the dribbling player and always behind her. They attempt to tackle the ball from their trapping- shielding-dribbling opponent. They too are constrained to move only in a line parallel to the other lines; they must never get in front of or alongside of the player with the ball. Their pressure is applied to the rear of each dribbler. This may seem somewhat artificial, but without this added constraint of not allowing them to get alongside of or in front of the trapping player, the trapping player would not receive and trap the ball very frequently during this drill. Greater and more realistic opposition pressure is introduced in the monkey-in-the-middle drill. As in the above drill, the player doing the trapping must go to meet the ball, and the defender is to stay behind this player at all times. After trapping the ball, the trapper backs up towards the line while shielding the ball. This player then dribbles along the line in the same manner as in the drill above, except that shielding is used to protect the ball. Every four minutes the dribbling and the attacking players are to switch positions.

Chest Trapping. This drill teaches effective chest trapping. The coach or knowledgeable players should demonstrate both the type in which the ball comes from the air to the chest and the type in which it comes from the ground to the chest. Split the players up into pairs and if there is an odd numbered player, that player should join a pair to form a threesome. They are to remain about 20' (6 meters) apart; 25' (7 ½ meters) apart for older players. Use field markers to keep the distance constant. They will take turns throwing the ball underhanded to their partner. The first portion of the drill is performed by throwing the ball in the air.

The ball is to be properly chest trapped so that it drops downward to the feet. Immediately after the chest trap, this player is to make a few dribbles in any direction for conditioning the players to accelerate immediately with the dribbled ball after it is brought under control with the feet.

The second portion of the drill is chest trapping a bouncing ball. This time the throw is made by throwing the ball overhanded at the ground so that it bounces up towards the chest of the trapper. After this trap is made, the player is again to make a few dribbles in any direction prior to kicking the ball back to the thrower.

Body Trapping. This drill teaches the effective use of the body to control a loose bouncing ball. There should be a few demonstrations of this trap to clarify its intent prior to commencement of the drill. The ball is thrown nearly straight up in the air to the trapper. After the ball takes its first bounce, the trapper gets behind the ball and aligns himself with its path. The trapper then pushes the ball with any portion of the body that is legal in soccer in some preferred direction of open space on the playing field. The trapper continuously shields the ball while endeavoring to get it under control with his feet. This person may chase the ball for 30' to 40' (9 to 12 meters) before getting it under close dribbling and shielding control. Pair off teammates to practice this drill. An odd player should join a pair to form a three-some.

DRIBBLING

The dribbling drill for young players is made into a contest. In this drill, it is not necessary, but it is recommended that the players touch the ball with each step as in other dribbling drills. Form two parallel lines of players about 10' (3 meters) apart. Place a field marker at the head of the lines. Ten feet (3 meters) in front of each marker, place another marker and place four more in succession 5' (1.5 meters) apart. The first player at the head of each line has a ball. After a signal, the players dribble the ball up to and around their markers (zigzag). They must dribble through each space between the markers; if a player misses a marker, he must go back. When the player returns and faces the starting line, he passes the ball to the succeeding player on his team. The winning team of each trial is the one that finishes first. The first team to win two out of three contests is the winner.

SHOULDER CHARGING

This is a drill that teaches nonaggressive players the controlled aggression that is legal in soccer and is discussed in Chapter 1. To practice shoulder charging, two individuals make bodily contact with their shoulders. The charging goes like this: If player 1 is dribbling the ball, player 2 runs alongside this player and uses her shoulder to dislodge player 1 from the ball. This may only be done if player 1 is dribbling the ball and it is near her. Shoulder charging is illegal if the ball is more then a few feet [about a meter] in front of the dribbler. It is also illegal to come up behind a player and shoulder charge from behind. Inexperienced referees will often call a foul against a legal shoulder charge, but the referee's error should not stop your players from using this technique.

The drill is performed as follows: Form two parallel lines of players about 3' (1 meter) apart. The ball is thrown out about 10' (3 meters) in front of both lines. Both players in front of the line run to try to win the loose ball and maintain its possession. The players are to run in a straight line to a field marker 100 yards (90 meters) from the lines of players. While the player with the ball is dribbling, the other player is shoulder charging (slightly bumping and pushing the other player with the shoulder) to dislodge the dribbler from the ball. After the second player "wins" the ball, she continues to dribble toward the marker. The shoulder charging should continue to the marker and back to the line with a continuous alternation taking place between the dribbler and shoulder charger, with at least two turns each. It is an important aspect of this drill to remember that the players are not to dominate each other. The idea is to have each player alternate as a shoulder charger and a dribbler a few times with each drill. If the dribbler outpaces the shoulder charging player, she should be told to slow down the pace and allow the shoulder charger an opportunity to dislodge the ball. At the end of each cycle, the players join the ends of the opposite line. The drill should continue until each player gets three or four repetitions.

DRIBBLING FEINT

The primary purpose of this drill is to instruct each player on the use of a dribbling feint. The secondary purpose is to teach a scoring technique against the goalkeeper. This drill also utilizes other techniques. For more information, refer to "Dribbling" and "Defending" in Chapter 3 and "Fakes" in Chapter 4. Line the players up as shown in Figure 6-6. The first few players in the line will have a ball. The coach will be about 10' (3 meters) in front of the goalkeeper, who in turn will be about 5' (1½ meters) in front of the goal. The players are about 40' to 50' (12 to 15 meters) in front of the coach, who is the defender. This is quite an important drill and should be practiced several times each season.

As the defender, the coach must vary the defensive pressure from practically zero to that encountered in a real game situation, depending upon the skill level of the players. When young players are learning this technique, you, the coach, should stand in place as a stationary

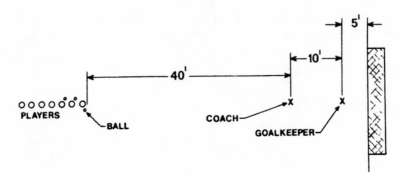

Figure 6-6. The lineup for the feint drill.

object as the attacker approaches with the ball; zero defensive pressure
is required for the novice players. Each player dribbles the ball with
the front of his preferred foot. For the sake of discussion, suppose the
player is using his right foot to dribble. As he comes within 4' (1.2
meters) of you, he slowly feints to the left and pushes the ball with the
right foot past you at a 45-degree angle. If the ball is kicked too hard,
the goalkeeper will get it. After the self-pass at 45 degrees, the player
must get a shot on goal with the first contact with the ball. The attacking player must not be allowed to play the ball a second time. The shot
is to be made on the laces of the shoe (the instep kick). If the ball is
not contacted with the laces of the shoe, the ball will miss the goal and
end up to the right of it. The ball must also be kicked at its midpoint
with respect to the ground to keep it from rising.

As the players improve their speed in both the feinting moves and
the self-pass, the defensive pressure can be increased up to a level sim-
ulating game pressure. It is important that the players realize that the
feint must look authentic; it should appear to the opponent that the
player is going in one direction, but he actually moves in the other
direction. After several practices, the players may be substituted into
the defending position. (See the defense drills below.) These players
must now run up to meet the attacker and then back up with this
player towards the goal. It is left up to the attacker when to feint, to
make a self-pass at 45 degrees, or to kick the low-elevated shot at the
goal. All players should have a chance to substitute for the defender
at least once in the season. The drill can be broken up into two or three
groups for more efficient practice.

Observe this drill carefully. Do not permit a feint to the left and a self-pass to the right using the left foot and vice versa. The body balance for this move requires that a pass to the right side (the self-pass) be made with the right foot, or a pass to the left side made using the left foot. As a reminder, when observing this and any other drill, be sure that it is done correctly, even if it is performed at a slow pace.

ONCE-ON

"Once-ons" in soccer usually refer to shots on goal when the ball is somewhere in front of the goal while rolling or bouncing on the ground. A header can also be included in this category. The player does not trap the ball but tries to score by kicking it directly into the goal. Another type of a once-on is kicking a volley shot at a goal as a low "air" ball. For our purposes of control-ball soccer training, only rolling balls and headers as air balls will be used for the once-on drills.

Once-ons are very inaccurate and should only be made at close range in front of the goal, not more than 25' (7 ½ meters) away. The soccer goal size seems large, but once-ons seldom get placed into the back of the net by amateur players, even when taken closer than 25' (7 ½ meters). The more the players practice at this drill, however, the more they will increase their chances of scoring. These drills are very useful as practice drills for warm-up before the game.

Rolling Ball. Line up your players on the right side of the field, about 100' (30 meters) from the goal and halfway between the imaginary line splitting the field lengthwise and the touch line. The coach should stand on the opposite side of the field, but about 35' (10 ½ meters) in front of the goal line as shown in Fig. 6-7. Push pass the balls (or roll them by hand for a more exact placement) across the goal mouth at an angle such that the first running player takes a shot about 20' (6 meters) in front of the goal. At this distance, the player should use the push pass. It is important to have the player start to run before you send her the ball. The idea is to beat the goalkeeper by having the players score as much as possible. This is required for positive reinforcement. Placing the ball further back may be your first impulse, but this will serve no useful purpose. Making it difficult to score must not be the objective of this exercise. It will only teach players how not to score. The goalkeeper will not like this exercise if it is performed correctly.

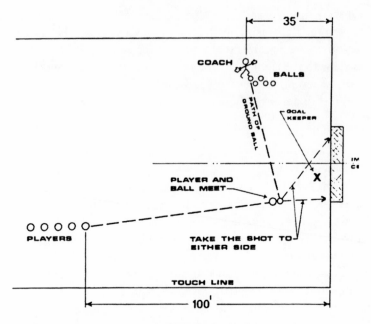

Figure 6-7. Once-on shots on goal drill.

After each player has been able to get five or six tries, switch to the left side of the field for another similar set of shots on goal where the passes come from the opposite direction.

Rolling Ball with Teammate, Variation 1. This drill is an important variation of the previous drill. It is intended to get attacking players in the habit of supporting attacks. With this drill, there is another parallel line of players alongside the first line of the original kicking players. These lines are placed about 20' (6 meters) apart. The players in this second line are to run towards the goal parallel to or slightly rearward of the player with the ball and thus participate in attacking the goal. Their job is to remain in a nonoffside position, yet be as close to the offside line as possible for the purpose of being in a strategic position should the ball become available there. In this variation, the original player with the ball takes the shot on goal.

Rolling Ball with Teammate, Variation 2. In this variation, using two lines of players as stated above, the ball is passed by the coach to the player coming from the furthest line from the coach (player 1), while player 2 remains in his line. The ball should reach player 1 about

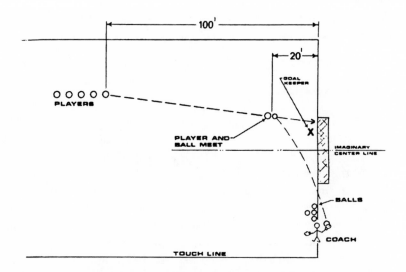

Figure 6-8. The heading once-on drill lineup.

40' (12 meters) from the goal line. Player 2 starts running towards the goal to receive the ball from player 1. Player 1 receives the ball from the coach and traps it dead at his feet. As player 1 is trapping the ball, player 2 should be running up to the imaginary line where player 1 is situated (parallel to the goal line) to receive a pass. When player 1 has control of the ball, he should make a push pass in front of player 2 ahead of this imaginary line. Player 2 must time his stride to meet the ball and make a once-on shot at the goal. The correct placement of the ball (the pass) must not be passed so close to the goal that it is within the goalkeeper's reach, nor should it be passed too far back so that player 2 must stop and wait to make the once-on shot at the goal. The shot should be made at about 25' (7.5 meters) in front of the goal.

Heading. Prior to executing this drill, it is recommended that the coach review "Heading" in Chapter 3. The heading once-on drill is performed in the same manner as described in the rolling ball drills section except that the coach's location is now back on the goal line. The players and coach are shown in location in Fig. 6-8. The first player on line runs in the direction of the goal, and the coach lobs the ball underhanded, preferably using both hands, to a point in front of this player such that the ball is just out of reach of the goalkeeper. For best results, the player should "get over the ball" to head it downwards, that is, hit the ball just above its midline. Placing the shot at the level of the goalkeeper's feet in outdoor soccer makes it a difficult save.

TRAP AND SHOOTING

Variation 1 Place the players about 75' (23 meters) on the imaginary, lengthwise center line back from the goalpost. The goalkeeper (or the coach, standing just to the side of the goal) throws the ball out toward the player running in to the goal. The young player must trap the ball dead at his feet about 25' (7 ½ meters) in front of the goal (slightly further out for older players). This player should then get his balance and take the shot as described in Chapter 4, "Trapping in Front of the Goal." The precise number of steps must be executed to perform this exercise correctly; no step is to be left out. Note that you should not make it difficult for the players to score by having them kick from great distances to the goal.

The thrower can throw the ball high, low, or any way he chooses as long as it can be reasonably controlled by the attacking player. Each player should do three of these shot-on-goal exercises because repetition is needed to attain a degree of proficiency. This drill is also an excellent one for the goalkeeper.

Variation 2 This variation uses the coach to feed the balls from the side of the attacking player instead of from the front of the goal. The coach stands 25' (7 ½ meters) from the goal line and halfway between the touch line and the imaginary center of the field line. The coach makes push passes to the player so that the ball and player arrive at about the penalty spot at the same time. Once again the player must go through all of the steps to execute the shot-on-goal correctly.

Variation 3 This advanced drill is a variation of the preceding one and utilizes a defender who is goalside of the receiving player. The receiver must employ shielding techniques while trapping the ball and must also make space for himself to get a shot-on-goal.

OTHER SCORING DRILLS

Variation 1 This drill is a contest between two lines of players with a single player at a time attacking on goal. Form two parallel lines about 50' (15 meters) in front of the goal. The players should be about midway between the touch line and an imaginary center line dividing the field. Before forming the two lines, balance each line (team) with equal talent and place a goalkeeper in front of the goal. The first player of each team has a ball. The second players should also have balls to speed up the drill. Each team (one at a time) attacks the goal by dribbling up to it and then takes a shot-on-goal as in a break-away situation. The type of kick to be made is the push pass for very young players or the under-the-foot instep kick or any other kick for older players. The ball must be retrieved by the player after the shot. The lines get four turns apiece. Switch sides of the line after each player has had two turns. After every player has had four shots (two shots from each side), the winning team will be the one with the most goals.

Variation 2 This drill is essentially the same as the preceding one, except it employs realistic defense with a defending person controlling each team. The defender against each team should be from the opposing team. Change the defender after each line of players has one turn. Place the stronger players toward the end of each line because the defender will become more experienced with each attack against her. Do this drill often, placing the team's actual defenders in this defending position most of the time. All players should get some experience at defending, however.

Variation 3 This drill teaches accuracy in shooting. The players remain stationary during it. Place two field markers on the ground 2' (0.6 meter) apart for the goal and form two lines about 5' (1 ½ meters) apart from each other. Place these lines 20' (6 meters) in front of the goal. At the head of the lines, place another field marker to keep the shooting distance constant. Each player remains behind the line marker and gets three shots in succession but must utilize only the type of kick specified for the drill, that is, the push pass, the instep kick, etc. The winning team is the one with the most goals.

CROSSING DRILLS

The Blind Cross. This drill setup is shown in Fig. 6-9. The player with the ball dribbles it down the right side of the field. The kick is made with the right foot as the player nears the touch line. The left foot is used for the cross on the other side of the field. To make the

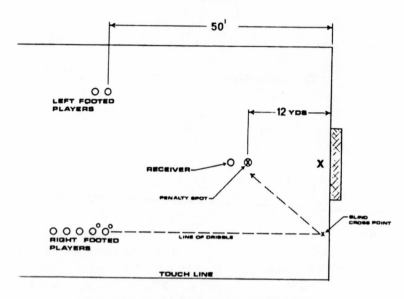

Figure 6-9. The blind cross air ball drill lineup.

blind cross, the ball must be pulled back in order to place it at the penalty spot.

This drill should be reserved for players at least ten years old because it is not normally effective for scoring goals by younger players for the following reasons: (1) They usually do not co-attack the goal when they are without the ball and thus are seldom in the right spot at the right time to score this way. (2) They usually cannot make good headers. (3) They cannot pull the ball back far enough to get it out of the goalkeeper's range — most crosses go directly to the goalkeeper. It is important to realize that the blind cross (or any cross for that matter) is in error if it goes directly to the goalkeeper. For details on the blind cross kick, refer to Chapter 7.

The Nonblind Cross. The nonblind cross should be preferred over the blind cross because the targeted individual remains in view up to the time of the kick. Another reason that this type of cross is effective is that the defender is usually goalside of the dribbler as this dribbling player heads inward toward the goal. The kicking foot is somewhat shielded from the defender because the kick is made toward the kicker's right side (the defender's left side). A left-footed shot made on the left side of the goal may be more easily blocked by a defender.

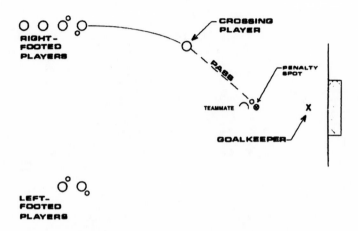

Figure 6-10. The nonblind cross drill lineup.

This kick was also discussed in Chapter 4 in "General Attacking and Defending." The procedure is as follows: (1) Place the right-footed players on the left side of the field and the left-footed players on the right side of the field. (See Fig. 6-10.) Have each player dribble the ball down the side of the field along the touch line starting at about midfield. About 25 yards (23 meters) from the touch line, have the player run inward toward the penalty spot and then kick the ball to the penalty spot using the basic instep kick or the inside-of-the-foot pass, which were both discussed in Part I of Chapter 3. There is also a teammate placed at the penalty spot. This player must trap ground balls dead at his feet before taking the shot or head the ball if it arrives in the air. (In an actual game situation, this player would be offside if there were no defender closer to the goal than he was.)

Crossing exercises are time consuming because you should substitute the receiver only after he receives about 20 crosses is a row. You may choose to have only the forward players receive the ball in this drill.

Wall Passing

The wall pass is discussed in Chapter 4. It is only recommended for players at least 14 years old. This self-pass is useful to pass a lone opponent when your team has a two-to-one player advantage at that

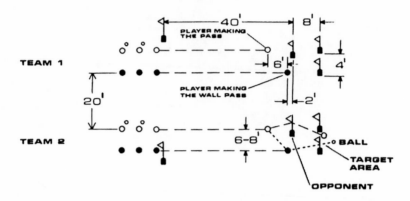

Figure 6-11. The wall pass drill lineup.

point on the field, along with ample space to make this play. Splitting up the players into two competing teams will make this drill interesting. Form four parallel lines of players as shown in Fig. 6-11. The right two lines form team 1, and the left two lines form team 2. Balance the talent in both teams. To follow the discussion, refer initially to team 1 in the figure.

This drill promotes teamwork as follows: The player with the ball (unfilled circle) dribbles the ball to a position approximately 6' (1.8 meters) in front of the "opponent" (the flag marked "opponent" as illustrated with team 2). At this point, the player making the pass (unfilled circle) passes the ball to his teammate (the player acting as the wall, a filled circle). This teammate then makes a wall pass using the push pass into the target area. The original player (unfilled circle) runs into the target area and traps and controls the ball, thus completing the play. Each team that is successful in correctly making this play is awarded a point. Each team gets four wall passes per player (a repetition of four times). After the team has used all players, the lines are switched to repeat this drill for the players previously acting as the wall. The team with the highest number of successful passes is the winner.

SHIELDING

See Fig. 6-12. This drill (the monkey-in-the-middle) is very effective for teaching basic shielding, but it is only effective if the rules are strictly enforced by the coach. It will degrade into a gang-up of

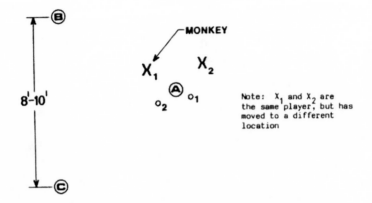

Figure 6-12. The monkey-in-the-middle drill lineup.

players A, B, and C against player X (X = the monkey = player X_1 = player X_2) when it gets out of control. The rules are as follows:

1. Any player (circled A, B, and C) must dribble and shield the ball four or five times before passing it off. Note in the figure the position of the monkey (X_1) and player A controlling and shielding the ball. Assume the position of the ball is o_1, so it is shielded from the monkey still located at position X_1. Now suppose the monkey tries to move closer to the ball, which is still in position at o_1, and in doing so he goes to position X_2. Player A then moves the ball to position o_2 to continue shielding it from the monkey.

2. The player with the ball is to make a pass only to the player who is furthest from the monkey's body (the safest pass to make). Continuing with the preceding example, we see that player A can only safely pass the ball to player C. If the ball, which is still located at o_2, is passed to player B, the pass might be successful, but if the monkey stretches his leg towards player B, a possible interception could take place. The interception from player B could also take place if player B made a poor trap. The only player completely unmarked is player C, who gets the pass. Prior to the pass, player A should dribble the ball four or five times.

3. The players must stay in an equilateral triangle 8' to 10' (2 ½ to 3 meters) maximum on a side.

4. When one of the A, B, or C players makes a bad pass or loses the ball, that player becomes the monkey. If no mistakes are made, the players are to switch the monkey every two minutes.

Run this drill approximately fifteen minutes.

DEFENSIVE DRILL

This is a very important drill for field players. As stated earlier in this book, if the teams are well matched, about 50 percent of the game will be on defense unless your team's pressure can reduce this figure. It is best to utilize this defensive time to your advantage, but it is going to be a function of the physical condition of the players. If they are in excellent physical condition, they can apply sufficient pressure to reduce their opponent's time in your defensive area and will take possession of the ball more frequently in or near the opponent's defensive area. This also conserves energy when your team is attacking the opponent's goal as they will have to run a shorter attack distance.

This exercise is conducted similarly to the feint drill: The attacking player starts at the center circle and dribbles down the center of the field toward the goal. The defending player rushes up to meet the attacker and then stops and backs up with the player as described in "Defending" in Chapter 3. The defending player backs up in such a manner as to avoid being "faked." The defender finally slows down to a halt about 10' (3 meters) in front of the goal. The defensive idea here is to remain goalside of the attacker at all times. While backing up, it is preferable to steer the attacker out towards one of the wings.

The idea is also to allow a shot on goal in such a way as to obstruct the attacker from having a clear shot and to allow the goalkeeper to make a predetermined estimate of the direction of the shot. Two defenders (one being the goalkeeper) working in unison have a distinct advantage over a single attacking player. If the defender makes the capital defensive error (going for the ball) and gets "beaten," however, then it is not a difficult task to also beat the goalkeeper. Executing this defensive move in game play correctly forces the opposition to make hasty passes that are quite often intercepted.

It is necessary to repeat a caution. At local level soccer, very few people understand the principle behind this noncommittal defensive move. It will most probably be necessary to caution spectators against yelling "get the ball" at players. This is not only distracting, but gives them a confusing message. It takes an experienced person to understand that this is the proper way to defend. If you are also apprehensive about the backing-up principle, observe experienced opponents who are easily passing your "star-attack-type" players as these players

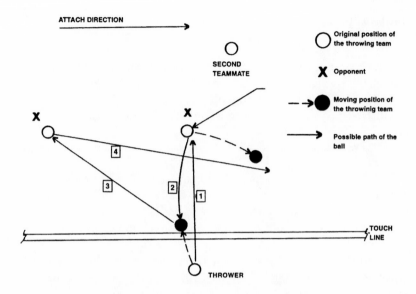

Figure 6-13. The throw-in drill lineup.

rush in to attempt to take the ball away. These observations should help to convince you of the soundness of this principle.

TWO AGAINST THE GOALKEEPER DRILL

This drill is described at the end of Chapter 5.

THROW-IN DRILLS

Throw-in drills are designed to instruct players that there is a definite method for maintaining possession of the ball when a throw-in occurs. Any haphazard throw-in method may turn the ball over to the opposition after three, four, or five touches on the ball. The players should be alerted to this.

Variation 1 Throw-Ins are discussed in Chapter 3. In this drill, five players are used. Three players (circles) take part in the throw-in, and two players act as opponents. (See Fig. 6-13.) Place the thrower along the touch line and the second teammate directly in front of him 15' (4½ meters) in the field. The third teammate is positioned as shown in the figure. Two opponents labeled X are behind the second and third teammates. The drill goes according to the following steps as shown in the figure:

1. From the touch line, the thrower throws the ball to the second teammate and then the thrower moves over the line into the field. This second teammate shields and traps the ball and possibly needs to balance by outstretching the arms (care must be taken not to obstruct the opponent).

2. The thrower calls for the ball back, and it is then passed back to him.

3. After the thrower gets the ball returned to him, he in turn passes it back to the second or third teammate, whichever player is more open.

4. The player with the ball then passes the ball to an unmarked teammate. The receiver could be either of the teammates, whichever is unmarked.

Note that this is a three-against-two situation, and the three players must develop the skill to keep the ball. All players receiving the ball are to shield it. Beating the two opponents by speed or any other means not described above will not teach the soundness of the tactic described above.

Variation 2 This variation employs a head pass. The thrower throws the ball to the teammate's head, and she in turn heads it back to the thrower's feet. The drill is then performed in the same manner as was the previous drill.

SUBSTITUTION OF ADVANCED TECHNIQUES INTO DRILLS

Drills of advanced techniques such as those in Chapter 7 can be substituted for drills that are described using elementary techniques. For example, the instep stride kick can be substituted for the instep kick and performed according to procedures described in the "Other Scoring Drills" section above. Note that it is preferable for any drill and its proficiency to be demonstrated by a person who knows how to perform them if they cannot be performed by the coach.

WASTE-OF-TIME DRILLS

Practice time is precious. There is never enough time for drills because there is so much to be learned, so do not use your time doing drills that offer no direct application to game situations. In my opinion, the following commonly used drills are not very efficient:

1. In one drill, two tandem columns of players face each other about 10 yards (9 meters) apart. The first player of column one kicks the ball to the first player of column two. This player in turn kicks the ball back to a third player in column one and so on. The ball is never under control. This exercise teaches no ball control or discipline.

2. In one dribbling drill, the players are allowed to dribble the ball as far out in front of them as they please. This exercise offers no disciplined dribbling techniques.

3. In the far-out, once-on drill, players are lined up beyond the penalty area to take long once-on shots-on-goal. The players seldom score at these distances, and this drill teaches them how not to score.

4. Corner kick drill. This exercise utilizes *kicked* corner-kicks with attacking players standing in front of the goal. Kicks are seldom accurate enough to utilize time efficiently. Possibly one out of three meets its mark. By contrast, throwing the ball is a much more consistent technique that allows for the exact placement of the ball nearly every time.

5. This is a goalkeeping exercise. The ball is thrown to the goal-keeper while he is sitting on the ground. This is a game of catch between the thrower and the goalkeeper that seems to be of little practical use.

6. Ball passing or rolling. This is an exercise in which all players roll the ball about their bodies with the apparent purpose of increasing sensitivity to the ball by increasing their contact with it. Field players have too little hand contact with the ball for this drill to be practical, however.

7. Advanced Techniques for Field Players

The techniques in this chapter are called advanced techniques, but they are probably no more difficult to learn than the basic skills. They are not as essential as basic skills but generally augment the experienced and well-disciplined player. If a league adopts the policy of teaching basic skills at the entry level and gradually introduces advanced techniques, it should develop above average teams and players for competition outside its own league. This chapter covers different advanced kicks, traps, and tackles to round the players out. It is important to remind the reader that players must master the basics of trapping and skills that control the ball with the inside of the foot as well as instep kicking, before advancing into this section.

It is suggested that the league officers rate the present level of play at two age-level cutoffs. If age groups 10 and older are still performing at a level of poor soccer and age groups 14 and older are performing only at an intermediate level, then a remedial program should be instituted to get the basics into effect. This type of program is simple in theory, but difficult to implement totally because of a resistance by coaches insisting that players trap the ball under pressure. Gradual changes can be made, however, by introducing coaches' clinics run by an individual who has a good understanding of how basic skills build winning individuals and teams.

In addition to considering the negative aspects of soccer, interested parents and league officers should draw a comparison between their players and professional teams that use ball control style of play.

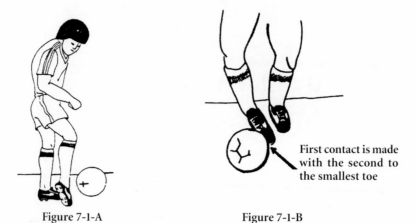

Figure 7-1-A   Figure 7-1-B

Figure 7-1. The outside-of-the-foot kick. Notice the position of the ball in Fig.
7-1-A. It is just in front of the nonkicking foot, which is 6" to 12" (15 to 30 cm)
from the ball. In Fig. 7-1-B, notice that there is a sweeping motion with the foot.

The comparison can be made by observing high level games on TV. It
is hoped that the impetus to watch such games does not come only
after your traveling teams return nonvictorious.

The previous discussion is necessary to help prevent coaches from
jumping into the advanced skills prematurely, but if basic skills are in
place, we can proceed to advanced skills.

Kicks

OUTSIDE-OF-THE-FOOT KICK

This kick is extremely useful for scoring goals and making passes
from your left side if you are a right-footer. For this discussion, we will
assume that the kicker is normally a right-footed kicker. For a left-
footed kicker, the exact opposite applies to the method for kicking.
The outside-of-the-foot kick enables a player to utilize a preferred
foot, even though it is advisable for a player to learn to kick with both
feet. For the right-footed kick, the ball is in front of the left foot, that
is, just to the left side of the body midline. (See Fig. 7-1 for the correct positioning of the feet.) Notice the position of the nonkicking left
foot. This kick is made when the ball is in front of the left foot; the

Photo 5. The outside-of-the-foot is used for making a pass to a player on the right of the kicker but not in view of the camera. Notice the sweeping motion of the foot.

left foot will be approximately 6" to 12" (15 to 30 cm) directly behind the ball. The right-footed kick will cause the ball to spin clockwise, thus curving it to the right. If this kick is used to curve the ball around a wall, the nonkicking left foot should be positioned on the left side of the ball and the toe of this shoe should be placed on the ground approximately at the vertical center-line of the ball. The second smallest toe of the kicking foot (right foot) should be the first to make contact with the ball. The camera illustrates this kick a split second after the impact of the foot with the ball in Photo 5. Note for comparison that in the angled instep kick the toes of the nonkicking foot are even with the front of the ball. With a right-footed kick, the angled instep kick spins the ball counterclockwise, and therefore curving it to the left.

MORE ABOUT THE ANGLED INSTEP KICK

Because the outside-of-the-foot kick has just been discussed and explained and it is useful for making a right-footed kick when the ball is on the left side of the body, a comment should be made for comparison with the angled instep kick. The angled instep kick is useful for making a kick with the left foot when the ball is on the left side

Figure 7-2. The under-the-body instep kick. Note the nonkicking foot is 6" to 12" (15 to 30 cm) away from the ball. The nonkicking knee is bent, the ball is contacted with the instep, and the kicking foot moves parallel to the ground.

of the body. This set of kicks enables a player to kick the ball with the same foot when it is on either side of the body. (See Fig. 7-2.)

These kicks can be made from the left or right side of the body, but we still need a kick to use when the ball is located near the center of the body. That is the subject of the next kick.

Duck-Bill Instep Kick

This kick is used when the feet are larger than size 8 and the ball is directly in front of the player's right foot, near the midline of the body. It is called a duck-bill kick because it is performed with the section of the foot just above the toes that is like a duck bill. This kick is performed in the same manner as the basic instep kick, with the nonkicking foot placed alongside the ball, except that contact is made near the toes instead of at the laces of the shoe. If the ball is kicked in its center, no spin or curvature should be observed.

Under-the-Body Instep Kick

The most common kick used by young players employs the instep. It is performed in the following manner by a right footer: The ball is

Figure 7-3. The front-volley and half-volley kicks.

pushed about 5' to 10' (1 ½ to 3 meters) to the right and in front of the kicker at about 30 degrees. The player then runs up to meet the ball and kicks it as shown in Fig. 3-10-C (the modified instep kick). This method is effective when the attacker is much faster than the defender or when a defender stabs for the ball and is beaten by the attacker. When defending players mature, however, they are not as prone to let attackers get off unimpeded shots with this type of kick. In essence, if players do not learn to modify this kick, they will find that they will be scoring fewer and fewer goals or getting the ball taken away when playing against competitive defenders.

The under-the-foot instep kick is a variation of the basic instep kick and allows players to kick the ball from under the body. In order to perform this kick smoothly, the nonkicking leg must squat and the nonkicking foot will be in its normal position for this type of kick (the toes are to be at the front of the ball), with the exception that this non-kicking foot is now about 6" to 12" (15 to 30 cm) to the side of the ball.

This squatting allows the instep to connect at about the center of the ball. Of course, the kicking foot is still angled as shown in Fig. 3-10-C. The kicking foot follows a straight line to the target and follows a path parallel to the ground; this kick is illustrated by a left-footed kicker in Fig. 7-2.

FRONT-VOLLEY AND HALF-VOLLEY KICKS

The volley kicks can be used to score goals when the ball is coming toward the attacker who is facing the opponent's goal. They can also be used to clear the ball in the dangerous area in front of the defender's own goal. All vollies require precise timing and balance. A normal occurrence is to see a volley that has been kicked at a goal end up in the treetops behind it. It also may be kicked so far from the side of the goal that nearly everyone watching is amazed by the inaccuracy as well as the velocity that the ball attains.

The half-volley kick is performed identically to the front-volley kick. The ball is struck with the foot in the same manner as a ball is struck with a bat. The difference is that the half-volley kick is kicked immediately after a bounce. For these volley kicks, refer to Fig. 7-3. The following rules apply:

RULE 1. Keep your eye on the ball. This applies during both the kick and the follow-through.

RULE 2. Position yourself directly behind the ball and not off to one side.

RULE 3. Wait for the ball to drop to a height of about 6" (15 cm) above the ground to kick a front-volley. For the half-volley, wait until the ball bounces about 3" (8 cm) above the ground before making the kick.

RULE 4. With your body over the ball, kick parallel to the ground for goal scoring shots. For clearance from the goal area, kick with a slightly elevated angle. In indoor soccer, the best location for the shot is the upper corner, and for outdoor soccer, the best location for the shot is the lower corner.

RULE 5. After the kick, follow up with the kicking foot moving in a straight line (do not make this kick with an arc motion of the leg).

One of the difficult aspects of volley kicks is in timing. The kicker must wait for the ball to drop to the correct height but when a ball is dropping, its velocity is difficult to judge because of its increasing downward speed. Much practice is needed to perfect the volley kicks. This kick is not recommended if the ball is further than 25' (7 ½ meters)

Figure 7-4. The side-volley kick. The knee of the kicking leg is at the same height as the ball.

out from the goal. Very few goals are scored in amateur soccer with a volley for the following reasons: a player does not get behind the ball, he does not let it drop sufficiently or there is insufficient time to execute the kick correctly because of opponent pressure. Beyond 25' (7 ½ meters), the trap and shoot method is recommended for the shot. The other alternative is to pass the ball to an open teammate.

SIDE-VOLLEY KICK

This kick is made with the knee at the same height as the ball. Like the front-volley kick, it must be practiced repeatedly to get the timing correct because the dropping ball is increasing its downward velocity. See Fig. 7-4 for the correct positioning of the body at the time the kick is executed. For the side-volley, the following rules apply:

RULE 1. Keep your eye on the ball during the kick and during the follow-through.

RULE 2. Turn the body 90 degrees to the direction from which the ball is approaching.

RULE 3. Pick up the kicking leg having the knee at the same height as the ball.

RULE 4. Kick from the knee, that is, with the knee bent 90 degrees prior to the kick. Hit the ball with the instep. Note that if the kick causes the ball to be propelled downward with little speed, your timing was based upon an assumed constant dropping speed of the ball. Kick sooner in this case, remembering that the ball is gaining speed as it drops.

Scissors Kick

The scissors kick always looks good whenever the occasion to use it arises, but goals are seldom scored with this kick because the ball is kicked back blindly. Its use is limited in controlled-ball soccer and therefore not recommended. If the player is interested in this type kick, several soccer books at the local library will adequately describe it.

There is a serious drawback to this kick that should be pointed out to the reader. If a backwards volley is performed near another player, it will most likely be called a dangerous play. What is worse, however, is that it can seriously harm another player because it is performed at the face and jaw level.

Blind-Cross Kick

This kick is important at older age-group levels. It is not recommended for younger players because their crosses in the air seldom lead to a goal. The younger players should cross the ball on the ground.

The blind-cross kick is usually performed by the forward winger or the player acting as the forward winger at that moment. (The left winger could have dribbled the ball back to her left half back's position. The left half back in turn overlaps into the left winger's position.) In either case, the left-winger having received the ball is now at the forward position. Suppose that this player is running down the wing near the touch line and decides to cross the ball in the air using the left foot to place the ball in front of the opponent's goal. It is hoped that she has a teammate within head-striking distance to head the ball into the net. It is not easy to make an effective cross, but the procedure is explained as follows:

The blind cross is often performed blind because the ball is kicked with the right foot from the right side of the field or with the left foot from the left side of the field. The kicker cannot see the targeted teammate at the time of the kick because an effective cross must be effected

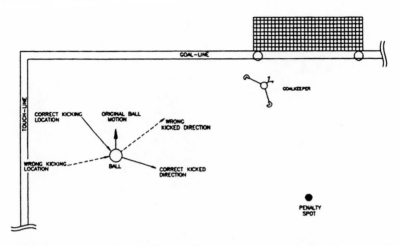

Figure 7-5. The wrong and the correct cross. The ball is often kicked at the wrong location and consequently ends up directly in the goalkeeper's hands.

approximately 90 degrees to 110 degrees from the kicker's direction of run.

The difficulties of making effective crosses from inexperienced wingers to inexperienced teammates must be overcome with self-discipline and training. For example, an inexperienced player may make a beautiful run down the wing and then attempt to cross the ball to the penalty spot, but instead of ending up at the penalty spot, it ends up directly placed to the goalkeeper. In a situation of this nature, inexperienced coaches do not help with a compliment such as "good effort." It is not a good effort because this attack was probably started as far back as your defending goal by one of your defensive players or the goalkeeper. All ten of your players may have run full speed downfield during this attack. Then a cross was kicked directly into the goalkeeper's hands. This bad cross just wasted the precious energy of all of your players. Now suppose that the opposing goalkeeper kicks the ball back to the half line. Your players all run back again. Your needed edge for another effective attack is lost when your enervated players are once again attempting to score against rested defenders. A full-scale attack may give your team only one try at the goal, so make the most of it by impressing upon the wing players that the only good cross is one that goes to one of these three places: The primary spot is the penalty spot if your forwards are nearby to keep the goalkeeper

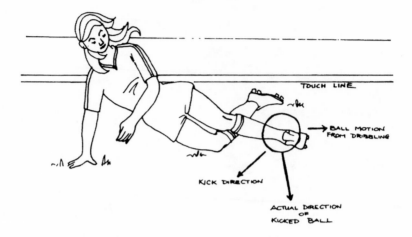

Figure 7-6. The blind-cross kick. Note the ball is actually kicked in a direction opposite to the dribbling direction.

back toward the goal. The second best spot is the near-post area. The goalkeeper may be close to the far post. The third choice can be the far post if the goalkeeper is not near it.

How is the direction of the ball rotated back between 90 degrees and 110 degrees from a position near the goal line? The following explanation is illustrated by Fig. 7-5.

The player must get her foot ahead of the ball's movement when kicking it. The point where the foot meets the ball is approximately 65 to 75 degrees from the rear of the ball (that point closest to one's own defending goal). Note in the figure that even if the ball is kicked at the "wrong kicking location," it does not follow that line of the kick because of its forward motion. The direction that the ball takes is some angle inbetween the ball's "original motion" arrow and the "wrong kicking location's" arrow. The exact angle is dependent upon the ball's original velocity and the force of the kick.

The method for crossing the ball with an angle greater than 90 degrees is to kick in front of the ball as shown in Fig. 7-6. The front of the foot actually misses the front of the ball, but the instep (lace of the shoe) catches the ball in such a manner that the kick should place it back to approximately 135 degrees. Because of the ball's forward speed (and the force of the kick), however, it will cross at an angle a little greater than 90 degrees relative to the direction of the run along the touch line. It must be mentioned that the longer the dribbler maintains possession of the ball, the closer she gets to the goal line. The closer one gets to the goal line, the greater the angle must become in order that the crossed ball be kept out of the goalkeeper's range. In the figure, the player is actually on the ground supported with the right hand and right calf as this cross is performed. When inexperienced players make this type of cross without going to the ground, the ball is often propelled with a very high trajectory. At higher levels of soccer, players often remain on their feet, however.

The following rules apply to the blind-cross kick:

RULE 1. Keep your eye on the ball during the kick and during the follow-through.

RULE 2. Cut the ball off by kicking it with the laces of the shoe in a way that will put it in a backwards direction from the dribble.

RULE 3. As the foot contacts the ball with the laces of the shoe, you are contacting the ground with the palm of the opposite hand from the kicking foot. It is repeated once again that experienced players often do not need to end up on the ground, but it is advisable as well as useful to learn the method described here.

RULE 4. The kick should be just below the midline of the ball from the ground level, and the resultant kick should follow a path parallel to the ground. This will cause the ball to rise slightly.

BACK-HEEL KICK

This kick is usually used to fake an opponent. When an attacker with the ball is under pressure from an opponent and the attacker knows that a teammate is behind him, a back-heel pass can be effective to confuse the opponent. It is a pass that must be practiced with teammates; otherwise they may not expect this pass during games and the effect of surprise will be lost, thereby negating the play. This kick is made by simply kicking the ball with the back of the heel while running and looking forward.

INSTEP-STRIDE SHOT

This is not actually a kick. It is a placement of the ball to the goal when running toward the goal. It is a part of the dribbling stride. As

Figure 7-7. The toe poke. This kick is useful when the attacker is "one-on-one" against the goalkeeper. This shot must be kept on the ground.

the ball is dribbled, it is pushed with the instep as shown in Figs. 3-10-B or 3-10-C. The next contact with the ball is again with the same instep, but this time the dribbling foot pushes the ball toward the target. If the ball is not directly in line with the instep and target, the instep corrects the ball's direction as the foot moves forward. The "kick" is part of the run and effective for a surprise shot on goal. There are two rules that must be followed for its proper execution.

RULE 1. Keep your eye on the ball during the push and during the follow-through.

RULE 2. Let the push be part of the stride. Learn this slowly at first, then as the method of propelling the ball takes hold, gradually increase its speed and power.

There are two advantages to using the instep-stride shot which make it difficult to defend against: (1) A defender running alongside at the left side of the attacker cannot get his foot set to block the shot made with the right foot because there is no actual kick. The ball is pushed with the right foot while running forward. (2) The goalkeeper cannot see the shot being executed because there is no setting up for the kick.

TOE-POKE

This kick is useful for scoring goals when an attacker is one-on-one against the goalkeeper. As the attacker advances toward the

Figure 7-8. This figure illustrates the contact point dropping toward the bottom of the foot with the trap. It is made sooner (time-wise) than the basic inside-of-the-foot trap illustrated in Fig. 3-1-A.

goalkeeper and the goalkeeper advances toward the attacker, the attacker simply pokes the ball to either side of the goalkeeper (See Fig. 7-7). This kicked ball must be kept on the ground by poking it with the point of the foot. The ball does not need to attain much speed for scoring with this shot.

There are three rules to follow:

RULE 1. Keep your eye on the ball during the kick and during the follow-through.

RULE 2. Wait for the goalkeeper to be nearly within touching distance of the ball before poking it past him.

RULE 3. Kick the ball gently, with the toe to either side of the goalkeeper and along the ground.

CHIP KICK

This kick is not used very frequently, but there are times when it can be useful. It is a slow, lofted kick that can be used to pop the ball over the goalkeeper when she is playing too far out from the goal. It can also be used to pass the ball over an opponent's head. A player interested in learning the chip kick can refer to one of the many soccer books that cover this kick adequately.

Traps

MORE ABOUT THE INSIDE-OF-THE-FOOT TRAP

Figure 3-1-A shows the basic trapping technique using the inside-of-the-foot trap. This figure only illustrates trapping when the

Figure 7-9. Trapping high balls that are passing the player to either his right or left side. The player is facing 90 degrees from the direction of the flight of the ball.

ball has passed through the imaginary vertical centerline of the body, that is, if the player is facing 90 degrees from the direction of the oncoming ball, the trap is made after the ball passes through the centerline of the body. The ball will often have to be trapped and settled before it crosses the body centerline, however. In these instances, the contact point shown in Fig. 3-1-B drops down toward the arch because the trap is made sooner, as illustrated in Fig. 7-8. The further in front of you the ball is trapped, the more the bottom of the foot becomes that targeted area of contact.

This can be easily understood if you imagine yourself facing in a direction at a 90-degree angle from the path of the imaginary ball approaching you. As you trap this imaginary ball, you will see that the further in front of you that you contact the ball, the more the bottom of the foot is utilized. When the impact is felt, the ball should be controlled to drop nearly motionless by relaxing the foot, allowing it to recoil on impact. The trap should be made nearer the top of the ball to keep it from bouncing up in the air. Remember to keep your eyes on the ball while trapping it, otherwise it may pass under the trapping foot if the foot is too high above the ground.

A more sophisticated method for excellent ball control and

Figure 7-10. The under-the-foot trap. This trap is difficult to make when an opponent is near unless he is behind the trapper.

balance with this type of trapping is to jump off the ground just before the moment of impact. This is particularly effective in indoor soccer, where the ball will not take any unpredictable hops. The sensitivity of touch is increased by practicing this trap barefooted against a wall or stairs as long as all of the precautions discussed in Chapter 6 are taken.

Another variation on the inside-of-the-foot trap is to reach out and pick balls out of the air that are passing to the left or right side of the player. The player faces 90 degrees to the direction of the flight of the ball and uses the inside of the foot to make contact at the point shown in Fig. 3-1-A. This trap is illustrated in Fig. 7-9.

UNDER-THE-FOOT TRAP

This type of trap is useful when the ball is coming straight at the player and no opponents are near to apply pressure. Shielding the ball immediately after contact using this type of trap is difficult unless an opponent is directly behind the trapper. The ball is trapped (actually wedged) using the sole of the foot and the ground to stop its momentum. (See Fig. 7-10.) This trap can be used for ground balls or for balls that bounce immediately before making foot contact.

HEAD TRAPS

This type of trap is not often used because most young players do not know about it. Most players think that the head should be used only to propel the ball. Of course, propelling the ball is sometimes necessary when it is at head level, but with control-ball soccer it is

Figure 7-11. The head trap. Note that the eyes are on the ball, the head recoils, and the ball may take an upward flight after the trap. Also note the point of contact on the forehead.

more advantageous to trap the ball than to head it long distances. The ball must be brought down to the ground and at the player's feet for control after the head trap is made. (See Fig. 7-11.)

This trap follows the same rules that apply to heading, except that the head must recoil slightly as the impact is felt. This move will cause the ball to rise slightly and then drop at the trapper's feet. If an opposing player is near, the ball must be shielded by placing the body between the opponent and the ball as it drops. This trap is time-consuming because the player must wait for the ball to drop, so it is usually performed when an opponent is not too near. As the ball contacts the ground, the feet must bring it immediately under control because an opponent will usually be near at this point in time.

There is a variation on this trap that can sometimes be made in front of an opponent's goal. A volley kick can be made on the ball as it drops from the head before it ever reaches the ground. (See Fig. 7-3.)

SIDE-OF-THE-THIGH TRAP

This trap is made by a player when the ball is coming directly at him at a waist-high elevation either from the ground or the air. (See Fig. 7-12.) The body must be turned 90 degrees from the direction of the ball's flight. The eyes must always be kept on the ball during the

Figure 7-12. The side-of-the-thigh trap. The body is facing 90 degrees from the direction of the ball's flight.

entire trapping procedure, and the thigh must relax because the muscle tissue will play a large part in deadening the ball upon impact. (See Fig. 7-12 for this trap.) Remember that this trap is best made when the impact angle between the ball's flight and the thigh is 90 degrees.

TOP-OF-THE-THIGH TRAP

This trap is generally used when the ball is coming straight at the player and dropping rather sharply. The ball is usually coming from a medium or long distance. The player faces the oncoming ball directly and lifts the thigh parallel to the ground or at an angle of 90 degrees to the flight of the ball. At the moment of impact, the eyes must be on the ball and the thigh must recoil to absorb the impact. The ball will bounce above the thigh before dropping to the ground. It is important to have the ball hit on the center of the thigh. If this does not occur, the ball will deflect to the right or left side and the player will not be in a position to control it with his feet. (See Fig. 7-13.)

CALF TRAP

The calf trap is similar to the side-of-the-thigh trap, but the ball's flight is slightly lower to the ground. The body is facing about 20 degrees from the ball's flight direction. In order to have the ball drop

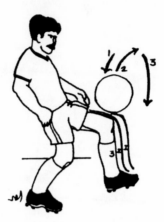

Figure 7-13. The top-of-the-thigh trap. After impact with the thigh, the ball rises slightly.

at the feet when making this trap, lift the leg slightly and let the ball meet the relaxed calf muscle. As the ball contacts the calf muscle, the leg relaxes and recoils with the ball. (See Fig. 7-14.) This trap is useful when you are approximately facing the ball and it is coming straight at you at an elevation of about knee level.

OUTSIDE-OF-THE-FOOT TRAP

The outside-of-the-foot trap is used when the inside-of-the-foot trap cannot be made. It is reserved for reaching or stretching for a ball that is at ground level but not coming directly at you. It should not be used when the ball is coming directly toward you because it will upset your balance. (When the ball is coming directly toward you, the inside-of-the-foot or under-the-foot trap should be used.) This trap is made by extending the foot so that the ball contacts the upper part of the toes. (See Fig. 7-15.)

DROPPING-BALL TRAP

As the name implies, the dropping-ball trap is used for trapping balls that are dropping nearly vertically. This trap is made by carefully following the flight of the ball and putting the trapping foot out under it in the same manner as using the tongue to catch a jelly bean. At the

Figure 7-14. The calf trap. The calf and foot of the trapping leg are turned 90 degrees from the direction of the flight of the ball. The body is turned about 20 degrees from the direction of the ball's flight.

moment of impact with the foot, however, the foot must be carefully withdrawn to follow the downward flight of the ball. This movement softens the impact to place the ball directly in front of the trapper. This trap is difficult to master because concentration on following the flight path is a must but is difficult under pressure, especially at the moment before contact. When mastered, however, this trap is useful and is a pretty sight to onlookers. (See Fig. 7-16.)

Pseudo Trap

The pseudo trap is one that is used extremely often by players in the prepractice warm-up. Before practice starts, early arrivals usually kick the ball back and forth to each other and use this trap. This trap brings the ball up in the air from the ground level. Effective traps in soccer bring the ball either downward or keep the ball down to be controlled by the feet. This pseudo trap is performed by letting the ball roll over the player's toes to permit it to pop straight up in the air. It is fancy, but probably useless in game play. The coach should prudently disallow this "trap" to be used in her presence to reinforce the point that ball control is a serious endeavor. Trapping where the ball drops dead or slightly in front of the trapper will only occur in game

Figure 7-15. The outside-of-the-foot trap. This trap should be used when the ball is coming straight at the trapper.

play if it becomes part of the disciplined player's techniques. Trapping must become reflexive (learned consciously and passed on to the subconscious). Using the pseudo trap or the wall pass which was discussed earlier and is also used too often in prepractice warm-ups, does not prepare soccer players for tough game pressure.

Tackles

Tackling methods are used to remove the ball from an opponent. Generally, there is no contact permitted with this tactic with the one exception of shoulder charging. In all tackles, the object is to dislodge the ball from an opponent. Tackles must be executed properly and with careful timing. With the exception of shoulder charging, after the ball is dislodged from the dribbler, it is then up to the player originally dribbling the ball to avoid the legs or feet of the tackling player. This constitutes a fair tackle, and the referee should not penalize the tackling player if the original dribbling player contacts the legs or feet of the tackling player after a fair tackle. Shoulder charging is a special case of tackling and is discussed in its own section.

STANDING-BLOCK TACKLE

This type of tackle is difficult for young players who instinctively go for the ball while the opponent has control over it. The standing-block

Figure 7-16. The dropping-ball trap. Prior to making this trap, the player must align himself directly in front of the approaching ball.

tackle requires patience, good balance, and proper timing in order for the tackling player to end up with the ball. As shown in Fig. 3-8, the defending player (the nondribbling player) is backing up with the dribbling player. The posture of the defender is to be on her toes with closed legs and to remain balanced to move quickly in any direction. The defender must then watch the ball and not the feinting moves of the dribbler. The only time that the defender makes a move for the ball is when the dribbler loses balance or dribbles the ball too far ahead.

At this moment the tackler places her foot firmly in front of the ball and supports it with the whole foot. (See Fig. 7-17.) The tackler then shifts her body weight more toward the ball, bearing even more support behind the ball. If the latter is not done, the dribbler will end up with the ball as he has sufficient forward momentum to overcome the weak resistance of the defender. If done properly, the defender will take possession of the ball.

SLIDING TACKLE

This tackle is the easiest to learn because its aim is to dislodge the ball from the carrier and slow up the attack. It is often effective when the opposing player is carrying the ball down one of the sidelines

Figure 7-17. The standing-block tackle. Notice the laces of the tackling foot are well positioned behind the ball to block its forward motion.

(touch lines). It may be executed with the purpose of kicking the ball over the touch line. This tackle is executed by coming at the dribbling opponent about 80 to 110 degrees from the direction she is traveling. It should not to be performed from the rear because a serious tripping foul could be the result of this tackle. If the player wanting to learn to make a sliding tackle already knows how to hook slide from baseball, then he already knows the technique. The point of contact on the foot is made with the toes. (See Fig. 7-18.)

When tackling by sliding in with the right foot, the left calf will be below the right calf at about a 70 to 90 degree angle and the calves will cross each other. The fall is broken by landing first on the left hand, then on the left forearm. The ball must be kicked firmly or the tackle will be unsuccessful. Reverse the movements for sliding in with the left foot. This tackle and the sliding-block tackle discussed next should only be utilized when another defender is backing up the tackling player. Otherwise, if the tackle is missed, the opponent is then unimpeded in front of the goal.

SLIDING-BLOCK TACKLE

This tackle is executed similarly to the sliding tackle, except that the nontackling leg is not bent. It is pulled back so that the ball can be

Figure 7-18. The sliding tackle. If the player contacts the ball and not the person, this tackle is legal. It is then up to the dribbler to avoid the tackler's foot or leg.

pinched with both feet. More time is needed to get to the ball and to execute the sliding-block tackle than is needed for the sliding tackle because the ball is blocked with the instep, just as with the standing-block tackle. The instep must be held firmly against the ball until the opponent's momentum carries him past the blocked ball. See Fig. 7-19 for the proper execution of this tackle.

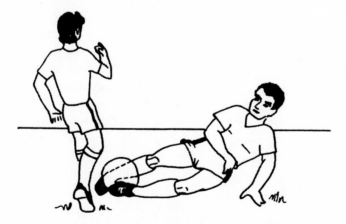

Figure 7-19. The sliding-block tackle. When the tackler contacts the ball and the opponent passes him, the tackler should pinch the ball with both feet to place it into position for making his next move.

Figure 7-20. The shoulder-charge tackle. The tackler has the advantage here because the shoulder-to-shoulder contact is distracting. The dribbler could maintain possession, however, if he decided to stop and shield the ball.

SHOULDER-CHARGE TACKLE

This tackle (often not called a tackle) is an effective method for dislodging the ball from the opponent. It has a strong psychological effect because it distracts the opponent. To be legal, the contact must only be shoulder-to-shoulder. It cannot be made from the rear of the opponent, and it must be made while the ball is near the opponent. Elbows and hips are not permitted in the contact. The most effective method for ending up with the ball after making opponent contact is to work the body between the dribbler and the ball, but only after taking possession of it. (See Fig. 7-20.) To do so before obtaining possession would violate Law XII, which concerns obstructing an opponent. When this maneuver is done properly, the tackling player will end up shielding and protecting the ball.

TWO-PERSON TACKLE

This tackle is made by two players either consciously or not consciously cooperating with each other. If player 1 is applying pressure on a dribbling player by running alongside or nearly alongside the dribbler, the dribbler is distracted. If the dribbler continues dribbling towards her opponent's goal, another teammate, player 2, approaches the dribbler. With two players now distracting the dribbler, the second opponent can usually move in and "sweep" the ball away from the dribbler.

Appendix: Laws
of the Game

The *Laws of the Game, Guide for Referees,* July 1995, has been repro-
duced with permission of the Fédération International de Football Associations (FIFA). They are the official laws of the International F.A. board.
FIFA is located at FIFA House, 11 Hitzigweg 11, Zurich, Switzerland, Tel:
41-1/384 9595.

A complete reference booklet of the *Laws of the Game,* including the
decisions of the International F.A. Board, may by purchased from the
United States Soccer Federation located at 1801 Prairie Avenue, Chicago,
Illinois 60166, Tel: 312-808-1300.

LAW I. The Field of Play

See Fig. 10-1

1. Dimensions. The field of play shall be rectangular, its length being
not more than 130 yards nor less than 100 yards and its breadth not more
than 100 yards nor less than 50 yards. (In international matches the length
shall be not more than 120 yards nor less than 110 yards and the breadth
not more than 80 yards nor less than 70 yards.) The length shall in all cases
exceed the breadth.

2. Marking. The field of play shall be marked with distinctive lines,
not more than 5 inches in width (not by a V-shaped rut) in accordance
with the plan, the longer boundary lines being called the touch-lines and
the shorter the goal-lines. A flag on a post not less than 5 ft. high and having a non-pointed top, shall be placed at each corner; a similar flag-post
may be placed opposite the half-way line on each side of the field of play,
not less than 1 yard outside the touch-line. A halfway-line shall be marked

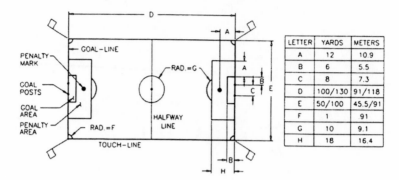

LETTER	YARDS	METERS
A	12	10.9
B	6	5.5
C	8	7.3
D	100/130	91/118
E	50/100	45.5/91
F	1	91
G	10	9.1
H	18	16.4

Figure 10-1.

out across the field of play. The centre of the field of play shall be indicated by a suitable mark, and a circle with a l0 yards radius shall be marked round it.

3. The Goal-Area. At each end of the field of play two lines shall be drawn at right-angles to the goal-line, 6 yards from each goal-post. These shall extend into the field of play for a distance of 6 yards and shall be joined by a line drawn parallel with the goal-line. Each of the spaces enclosed by these lines and the goal-line shall be called a goal-area.

4. The Penalty-Area. At each end of the field of play, two lines shall be drawn at right-angles to the goal-line, l8 yards from each goal-post. These shall extend into the field of play for a distance of l8 yards and shall be joined by a line drawn parallel with the goal-line. Each of the spaces enclosed by these lines and the goal-line shall be called a penalty-area. A suitable mark shall be made within each penalty area, l2 yards from the mid-point of the goal-line, measured along an undrawn line at right-angles thereto. These shall be the penalty-kick marks. From each penalty-kick mark an arc of a circle, having a radius of l0 yards, shall be drawn outside the penalty-area.

5. The Corner-Area. From each corner-flag post a quarter circle, having a radius of l yard, shall be drawn inside the field of play.

6. The Goals. The goals shall be placed on the centre of each goal-line and shall consist of two upright posts, equidistant from the corner-flags and 8 yards apart (inside measurement), joined by a horizontal crossbar the lower edge of which shall be 8 ft. from the ground.

For safety reasons, the goals, including those which are portable, must be anchored securely to the ground.

The width and depth of the crossbars shall not exceed 5 inches (l2 cm). The goal-posts and the cross-bars shall have the same width.

Nets may be attached to the posts, cross-bars and ground behind the goals. They should be appropriately supported and be so placed as to allow the goal-keeper ample room.

Goal nets. The use of nets made of hemp, jute or nylon is permitted. The nylon strings may, however, not be thinner than those made of hemp or jute.

LAW II. The Ball

The ball shall be spherical; the outer casing shall be of leather or other approved materials. No material shall be used in its construction which might prove dangerous to the players.

The circumference of the ball shall not be more than 28 in. and not less than 27 in. The weight of the ball at the start of the game shall not be more than 16 oz. nor less than 14 oz. The pressure shall be equal to 0.6-1.1 atmosphere ($=600$-1,100 gr/cm^2) at sea level. The ball shall not be changed during the game unless authorized by the referee.

LAW III. Number of Players

(1) A match shall be played by two teams, each consisting of not more than eleven players, one of whom shall be the goalkeeper.

(2) Up to a maximum of three substitutes may be used in any match played in an official competition under the auspices of FIFA, the Confederations or the National Associations.

The rules of competition shall state how many substitutes may be nominated, up to a maximum of five.

The names of the substitutes must be given to the referee prior to the commencement of the match.

Substitutes not so named may not take part in the match.

(3) In other matches, up to five substitutes may also be used provided that the teams concerned reach an agreement on the maximum number, and that the referee is informed before the match. If the referee is not informed, or no agreement is reached before the commencement of the match, no more than three substitutes shall be permitted.

The names of the substitutes must be given to the referee prior to the commencement of the match.

(4) Any of the other players may change places with the goalkeeper, provided that the referee is informed before the change is made, and provided also that the change is made during a stoppage of the game.

(5) When a goalkeeper or any other player is to be replaced by a substitute, the following conditions shall be observed:

(a) The referee shall be informed of the proposed substitution, before it is made.

(b) The substitute shall not enter the field of play until the player he is replacing has left, and then only after having received a signal from the referee.

(c) He shall enter the field during a stoppage in the game, and at the halfway line.

(d) A player who has been replaced shall not take any further part in the game.

(e) A substitute shall be subject to the authority and jurisdiction of the referee whether called upon to play or not.

(f) The substitution is completed when the substitute enters the field of play, from which moment he becomes a player and the player whom he is replacing ceases to be a player.

Punishment:

(a) Play shall not be stopped for an infringement of paragraph 4. The players concerned shall be cautioned immediately when the ball goes out of play.

(b) If a substitute enters the field of play without the authority of the referee, play shall be stopped. The substitute shall be cautioned and removed from the field or sent off according to the circumstances. The game shall be restarted by the referee dropping the ball at the place where it was when play was stopped, unless it was within the goal-area at that time, in which case it shall be dropped on that part of the goal-area line which runs parallel to the goal-line, at the point nearest to where the ball was when play was stopped.

(c) For any other infringement of this Law, the player concerned shall be cautioned, and if the game is stopped by the referee to administer the caution, it shall be restarted by an indirect free-kick, to be taken by a player of the opposing team from the place where the ball was when play was stopped, subject to the overriding conditions imposed in Law XIII.

LAW IV. Players' Equipment

(1) (a) The basic compulsory equipment of a player shall consist of a jersey or shirt, shorts, stockings, shinguards and footwear.

(b) A player shall not wear anything which is dangerous to another player.

(2) Shinguards, which must be covered entirely by the stockings, shall be made of a suitable material (rubber, plastic, polyurethane, or similar substance) and shall afford a reasonable degree of protection.

(3) The goalkeeper shall wear colors which distinguish him from the other players and from the referee.

Punishment:

For any infringement of this Law, the player at fault shall be instructed to leave the field of play by the referee, to adjust his equipment or obtain any missing equipment, when the ball next ceases to be in play, unless by then the player has already corrected his equipment. Play shall not be stopped immediately for an infringement of this Law. A player who is instructed to leave the field to adjust his equipment or obtain missing equipment shall not return without first reporting to the referee, who shall satisfy himself that the player's equipment is in order. The player shall only re-enter the game at a moment when the ball has ceased to be in play.

LAW V. Referees

A referee shall be appointed to officiate in each game. His authority and the exercise of the powers granted to him by the Laws of the Game commence as soon as he enters the field of play.

His power of penalizing shall extend to offenses committed when play has been temporarily suspended, or when the ball is out of play. His decision on points of fact connected with the play shall be final, so far as the result of the game is concerned. He shall:

(a) enforce the Laws.

(b) refrain from penalizing in cases where he is satisfied that, by doing so, he would be giving an advantage to the offending team.

(c) keep a record of the game; act as timekeeper and allow the full or agreed time, adding thereto all time lost through accident or other cause.

(d) have discretionary power to stop the game for any infringement of the Laws and to suspend or terminate the game whenever, by reason of the elements, interference by spectators, or other cause, he deems such stoppage necessary. In such a case he shall submit a detailed report to the competent authority, within the stipulated time, and in accordance with the provisions set up by the National Association under whose jurisdiction the match was played. Reports will be deemed to be made when received in the ordinary course of post.

(e) from the time he enters the field of play, caution and show a yellow card to any player guilty of misconduct or ungentlemanly behavior. In such cases the referee shall send the name of the offender to the competent authority, within the stipulated time, and in accordance with the provisions set up by the national association under whose jurisdiction the match was played.

(f) allow no person other than the players and linesmen to enter the field of play without his permission.

(g) stop the game if, in his opinion, a player has been seriously injured; have the player removed as soon as possible from the field of play, and immediately resume the game. If a player is slightly injured, the game shall not be stopped until the ball has ceased to be in play. A player who is able to go to the touch- or goal-line for attention of any kind, shall not be treated on the field of play.

(h) send off the field of play and show a red card to any player who, in his opinion, is guilty of violent conduct, serious foul play, the use of foul or abusive language or who persists in misconduct after having received a caution.

(i) signal for recommencement of the game after all stoppages.

(j) decide that the ball provided for a match meets with the requirements of Law II.

LAW VI. Linesmen

Two linesmen shall be appointed, whose duty (subject to the decision of the referee) shall be to indicate:
(a) when the ball is out of play,
(b) which side is entitled to a corner-kick, goal-kick or throw-in,
(c) when a substitution is desired.
They shall also assist the referee to control the game in accordance with the Laws. In the event of undue interference or improper conduct by a linesman, the referee shall dispense with his services and arrange for a substitute to be appointed. (The matter shall be reported by the referee to the competent authority.)

The linesmen should be equipped with flags by the club on whose ground the match is played.

LAW VII. Duration of the Game

The duration of the game shall be two equal periods of 45 minutes, unless otherwise mutually agreed upon, subject to the following:

(a) Allowance shall be made in either period for all time lost through substitution, the transport from the field of injured players, time-wasting or other cause, the amount of which shall be a matter for the discretion of the referee.

(b) Time shall be extended to permit a penalty-kick being taken at or after the expiration of the normal period in either half.

The half-time interval shall not exceed fifteen minutes.

Competition rules shall clearly stipulate the duration of the half-time interval.

The duration of the half-time interval may be altered only with the consent of the referee.

LAW VIII. The Start of Play

(a) At the beginning of the game, choice of ends and the kick-off shall be decided by the toss of a coin. The team winning the toss shall have the option of choice of ends or the kick-off. The referee having given a signal, the game shall be started by a player taking a place-kick (i.e., a kick at the ball while it is stationary on the ground in the center of the field of play) into his opponents' half of the field of play. Every player shall be in his own half of the field and every player of the team opposing that of the kicker shall remain not less than 10 yards from the ball until it is kicked-off; it shall not be deemed in play until it has traveled the distance of its own circumference. The kicker shall not play the ball a second time until it has been touched or played by another player.

(b) After a goal has been scored, the game shall be restarted in like manner by a player of the team losing the goal.

(c) After half-time; when restarting after half-time, ends shall be changed and the kick-off shall be taken by a player of the opposite team to that of the player who started the game.

Punishment:

For any infringement of this Law, the kick-off shall be retaken, except in the case of the kicker playing the ball again before it has been touched or played by another player; for this offense an indirect free-kick shall be taken by a player of the opposing team from the place where the infringement occurred, subject to the overriding conditions imposed in Law XIII.

A goal shall not be scored direct from a kick-off.

(d) After any other temporary suspension; when restarting the game after a temporary suspension of play from any cause not mentioned elsewhere in these Laws, provided that immediately prior to the suspension the ball has not passed over the touch or goal-lines, the referee shall drop the ball at the place where it was when play was suspended, unless it was within the goal-area at that time, in which case it shall be dropped on that part of the goal-area line which runs parallel to the goal-line, at the point nearest to where the ball was when play as stopped. It shall be deemed in play when it has touched the ground; if, however, it goes over the touch- or goal-lines after it has been dropped by the referee, but before it is touched by a player, the referee shall again drop it. A player shall not play the ball until it has touched the ground.

If this section of the Laws is not complied with, the referee shall again drop the ball.

LAW IX. Ball In and Out of Play

The ball is out of play:

(a) when it has wholly crossed the goal-line or touch-line, whether on the ground or in the air.

(b) when the game has been stopped by the referee.

The ball is in play at all other times from the start of the match to the finish including:

(a) if it rebounds from a goal-post, cross-bar or corner-flag post into the field of play.

(b) if it rebounds off either the referee or linesmen when they are in the field of play.

(c) in the event of a supposed infringement of the Laws, until a decision is given.

LAW X. Method of Scoring

Except as otherwise provided by these Laws, a goal is scored when the whole of the ball has passed over the goal-line, between the goal-posts and under the cross-bar, provided it has not been thrown, carried or intentionally propelled by hand or arm, by a player of the attacking side, except in the case of a goalkeeper, who is within his own penalty-area.

The team scoring the greater number goals during a game shall be the winner; if no goals or an equal number of goals are scored, the game shall be termed a "draw."

LAW XI. Off-Side

1. A player is in an offside position if he is nearer to his opponents' goal-line than the ball, unless:

(a) he is in his own half of the field of play, or

(b) he is not nearer to his opponents' goal-line than at least two of his opponents.

2. It is not an offense in itself to be in an offside position.

A Player shall only be penalized for being in an offside position if at the moment the ball touches, or is played by one of his team, he is, in the opinion of the referee, involved in active play by:

(a) interfering with play, or

(b) interfering with an opponent, or

(c) gaining the advantage by being in that position.

3. A player shall not be declared offside by the referee

(a) merely because of his being in an offside position or

(b) if he receives the ball direct from a goal-kick, a corner-kick or throw-in.

4. If a player is declared offside, the referee shall award an indirect free-kick, which shall be taken by a player of the opposing team from the place where the infringement occurred, unless the offense is committed by a player in his opponents' goal area, in which case the free-kick shall be taken from any point within the goal area.

LAW XII. *Fouls and Misconduct*

A player who commits any of the following offences in a manner considered by the referee to be careless, reckless or involving disproportionate force:

(a) kicks or attempts to kick an opponent; or

(b) trips an opponent; or

(c) jumps at an opponent; or

(d) charges an opponent: or

(e) strikes or attempts to strike an opponent; or

(f) pushes an opponent;

or who commits any of the following four offences:

(g) when tackling an opponent makes contact with the opponent before contact is made with the ball; or

(h) holds an opponent or spits at an opponent: or

(i) handles the ball deliberately, i.e., carries, strikes or propels the ball with his hand or arm, (this does not apply to the goal-keeper within his own penalty-area) shall be penalized by the award of a **direct free-kick** to be taken by the opposing team from the place where the offense occurred, unless the offense is committed by a player in his opponents' goal-area, in which case the free-kick shall be taken from any point within the goal-area.

Should a player of the defending team intentionally commit one of the above nine offenses within the penalty-area, he shall be penalized by a **penalty-kick**.

A penalty-kick can be awarded irrespective of the position of the ball, if in play, at the time an offense within the penalty-area is committed.

A player committing any of the five following offenses:

1. playing in a manner considered by the referee to be dangerous, e.g., attempting to kick the ball while held by the goalkeeper;

2. charging fairly, i.e., with the shoulder, when the ball is not within playing distance of the players concerned and they are definitely not trying to play it;

3. when not playing the ball, impeding the progress of an opponent, i.e., running between the opponent and the ball, or interposing the body so as to form an obstacle to an opponent;

4. charging the goalkeeper except when he

    (a) is holding the ball;

    (b) is obstructing an opponent;

    (c)has passed outside his goal-area.

5. when playing as a goalkeeper and within his own penalty-area:

    (a) from the moment he takes control of the ball with his hands, he takes more than 4 steps in any direction whilst holding, bouncing or throwing the ball in the air and catching it again, without releasing it into play, or

    (b) having released the ball into play before, during or after the 4 steps, he touches it again with his hands, before it has been touched or played by a player of the opposing team either inside or outside of the penalty area, or by a player of the same team outside the penalty area, subject to the overriding conditions of 5(c), or

    (c)touches the ball with his hands after it has been deliberately kicked to him by a team-mate, or

    (d) indulges in tactics, which in the opinion of the referee, are designed to hold up the game and thus waste time and so give an unfair advantage to his own team,

shall be penalized by the award of an **indirect free-kick** to be taken by the opposing side from the place where the infringement occurred, subject to the overriding conditions imposed in Law XIII.

A player shall be **cautioned and shown the yellow card** if:

    (j) he enters or re-enters the field of play to join or rejoin his team after the game has commenced, or leaves the field of play during the progress of the game (except through accident) without, in either case, first having received a signal from the referee showing him that he may do so. If the referee stops the game to administer the caution, the game shall be restarted by an indirect free-kick taken by a player of the opposing team from the place where the ball was when the referee stopped the game, subject to the overriding conditions imposed in Law XIII.

If, however, the offending player has committed a more serious offense, he shall be penalized according to that section of the law he infringed.

(k) he persistently infringes the Laws of the Game;

(l) he shows, by word or action, dissent from any decision given by the referee;

(m) he is guilty of ungentlemanly conduct.

For any of these last three offenses, in addition to the caution, an indirect free-kick shall also be awarded to the opposing side from the place where the offense occurred, subject to the overriding conditions imposed in Law XIII, unless a more serious infringement of the Laws of the Game was committed.

A player shall be **sent off the field of play and shown the red card,** if, in the opinion of the referee, he:

(n) is guilty of violent conduct;

(o) is guilty of serious foul play;

(p) uses foul or abusive language;

(q) is guilty of a second cautionable offense after having received a caution.

If play is stopped by reason of a player being ordered from the field for an offense without a separate breach of the Law having been committed, the game shall be resumed by an **indirect free-kick** awarded to the opposing side from the place where the infringement occurred, subject to the overriding conditions imposed in Law XIII.

LAW XIII. Free-Kick

Free-kicks shall be classified under two headings: "direct" (from which a goal can be scored direct against the offending side) and "indirect" (from which a goal cannot be scored unless the ball has been played or touched by a player other than the kicker before passing through the goal).

When a player is taking a direct or an indirect free-kick inside his own penalty-area, all of the opposing players shall be at least ten yards (9.15m) from the ball and shall remain outside the penalty-area until the ball has been kicked out of the area. The ball shall be in play immediately after it has traveled the distance of its own circumference and is beyond the penalty-area. The goalkeeper shall not receive the ball into his hands, in order that he may thereafter kick it into play. If the ball is not kicked direct into play, beyond the penalty-area, the kick shall be retaken.

When a player is taking a direct or an indirect free-kick outside his own penalty-area, all of the opposing players shall be at least ten yards from the ball, until it is in play, unless they are standing on their own goal-line, between the goal-posts. The ball shall be in play when it has traveled the distance of its own circumference.

If a player of the opposing side encroaches into the penalty-area, or within ten yards of the ball, as the case may be, before a free-kick is taken, the referee shall delay the taking of the kick, until the Law is complied with.

The ball must be stationary when a free-kick is taken, and the kicker shall not play the ball a second time, until it has been touched or played by another player.

Notwithstanding any other reference in these Laws to the point from which a free-kick is to be taken:

1. Any free-kick awarded to the defending team, within its own goal-area, may be taken from any point within the goal-area.

2. Any indirect free-kick awarded to the attacking team within its opponent's goal-area shall be taken from the part of the goal-area line which runs parallel to the goal-line, at the point nearest to where the offense was committed.

Punishment:

If the kicker, after taking the free-kick, plays the ball a second time before it has been touched or played by another player, an indirect free-kick shall be taken by a player of the opposing team from the spot where the infringement occurred, unless the offense is committed by a player in his opponent's goal-area, in which case the free-kick shall be taken from any point within the goal-area.

LAW XIV. Penalty-Kick

A penalty-kick shall be taken from the penalty-mark and, when it is being taken, all players with the exception of the player taking the kick, properly identified, and the opposing goalkeeper, shall be within the field of play but outside the penalty-area, and at least 10 yards from the penalty-mark and must stand behind the penalty mark.

The opposing goalkeeper must stand (without moving his feet) on his own goal-line, between the goal-posts, until the ball is kicked. The player taking the kick must kick the ball forward; he shall not play the ball a second time until it has been touched or played by another player. The ball shall be deemed in play directly after it is kicked, i.e., when it has traveled the distance of its circumference. A goal may be scored directly from a penalty-kick. When a penalty-kick is being taken during the normal course of play, or when time has been extended at half-time or full-time to allow a penalty-kick to be taken or retaken, a goal shall not be nullified if, before passing between the posts and under the cross-bar, the ball touches either or both of the goal-posts, or the cross-bar, or the goalkeeper, or any combination of these agencies, providing that no other infringement has occurred.

Punishment:

For any infringement of this Law:

(a) by the defending team, the kick shall be retaken if a goal has not resulted.

(b) by the attacking team other than by the player taking the kick, if a goal is scored it shall be disallowed and the kick retaken.

(c) by the player taking the penalty-kick, committed after the ball is in play, a player of the opposing team shall take an indirect free-kick from the spot where the infringement occurred, subject to the overriding conditions imposed in Law XIII.

LAW XV. Throw-In

When the whole of the ball passes over a touch-line, either on the ground or in the air, it shall be thrown in from the point where it crossed the line, in any direction, by a player of the team opposite to that of the player who last touched it. The thrower at the moment of delivering the ball must face the field of play and part of each foot shall be either on the touch-line or on the ground outside the touch-line. The thrower shall use both hands and shall deliver the ball from behind and over his head. The ball shall be in play immediately after it enters the field of play, but the thrower shall not again play the ball until it has been touched or played by another player. A goal shall not be scored direct from a throw-in.

Punishment:

(a) If the ball is improperly thrown in, the throw-in shall be taken by a player of the opposing team.

(b) If the thrower plays the ball a second time before it has been touched or played by another player, an indirect free-kick shall be taken by a player of the opposing team from the place where the infringement occurred, subject to the overriding conditions imposed in Law XIII.

LAW XVI. Goal-Kick

When the whole of the ball passes over the goal-line excluding that portion between the goal-posts, either in the air or on the ground, having last been played by one of the attacking team, it shall be kicked direct into play beyond the penalty-area from any point within the goal-area by a player of the defending team. A goalkeeper shall not receive the ball into his hands from a goal-kick in order that he may thereafter kick it into play. If the ball is not kicked beyond the penalty-area, i.e., direct into play, the kick shall be retaken. The kicker shall not play the ball a second time until it has touched or been played by another player. A goal shall not be scored direct from such a kick. Players of the team opposing that of the player taking the goal-kick shall remain outside the penalty-area until the ball has been kicked out of the penalty-area.

Punishment:

If a player taking a goal-kick plays the ball a second time after it has passed beyond the penalty-area, but before it has touched or been played by another player, an indirect free-kick shall be awarded to the opposing team, to be taken from the place where the infringement occurred, subject to the overriding conditions imposed in Law XIII.

LAW XVII. Corner Kick

When the whole of the ball passes over the goal-line, excluding that portion between the goal-posts, either in the air or on the ground, having last been played by one of the defending team, a member of the attacking team shall take a corner-kick, i.e., the whole of the ball shall be placed within the quarter circle at the nearest corner-flagpost, which must not be moved, and it shall be kicked from that position. A goal may be scored direct from such a kick. Players of the team opposing that of the player taking the corner-kick shall not approach within 10 yards of the ball until it is in play, i.e., it has traveled the distance of its own circumference, nor shall the kicker play the ball a second time until it has been touched or played by another player.

Punishment:

(a) If the player who takes the kick plays the ball a second time before it has been touched or played by another player, the referee shall award an indirect free-kick to the opposing team, to be taken from the place where the infringement occurred, subject to the overriding conditions imposed in Law XIII.

(b) For any other infringement the kick shall be retaken.

Index

advanced techniques 153
age *see* skill levels, by age
aggression 20-21
attack soccer 89
attacking 82

ball: control of 8, 14, 28, 90; laws
181; quality soccer 22; spin 63
body pushing 6
breakaway, goalkeeper 98, 116

cards, red and yellow 104–105,
107–110, 188, 189
center half back *see* half backs
charter *see* league, charter
child's playing time 17
clothing 23
coaches: beginning 26–27; clinic 25,
153; co-coaching 8; committee
33; control of 14–15; development
11, 12, 153
conditioning 21; *see also* stretching
control 13–16, 50; ball 1, 5, 14, 50,
51, 139
coordinator *see* orange designator;
referee; substitution coordinator
criticism: corrective or constructive
6, 18
crosses 7, 39, 75, 93, 94, 143–145,
160–163

defending 7, 12, 58, 61, 82
defense 8, 31, 39, 89, 148; errors 86;

lines of (or echelons of) 38, 39, 41,
60, 89, 111–112; play 31; positions
71; soccer 28, 38–39, 89; strategy
31, 86–89, 132; throw-ins 93; weak
71; *see also* half backs, center;
sweeper back; wingers, defensive
drawing off players 7, 20, 82, 100
dribbling 7, 29, 45–48, 50–54, 56,
128–129, 132, 133; caution 127, 167;
stepping on the ball, and 51, 54
drills, homework 127; dribble and
run 129; jump and ball bounce
129; precaution 129; rolling ball
130; sensitivity of touch 129; volley 128
drills, practice 28, 29, 139; body trap
139; caution 127, 167; chest traps
135; common sense 132; defensive
142, 143, 148; dribbling 136; feint
137; goalkeeper 22; goalkeeper
breakaway 126, 149; heading 49,
100, 141; monkey in the middle 52,
135, 146; once-on 100; rolling ball
140; scoring 142, 145; shielding
52; shoulder charging 136; soccer
28, 38–39, 89; strategy 31, 86–89,
132; substituting advanced techniques for basic drill methods 150;
throw-in 93, 149–150; trap and
shoot 100; volley 128; wall pass
145–146; warm up 21, 139; waste
of time 150–151

elements of the game 71
energy, conserve 148

equipment: first aid 23; game 22; personal 22; *see also* laws

fakes or feints 46, 96
FIFA (Fédération Internationale de Football Associations) 179, 181
formations 76; beehive 26; 4-3-3 formation 79, 82; 3-3-4 formation 80; 4-4-2 formation 80; 3-2-5 formation 81; w-m formation 73–74, 77–78
forwards: center 76, 80; wingers 73–76, 83, 94, 96

goalkeeper 7, 12, 15, 20, 41, 57–58, 60, 71, 72, 77, 83, 87, 89, 114, 182, 183; break-away 116, 125–126; catching 114, 120; deflecting 112; equipment 22; kicks 95, 123, 124, 192; lunging 121; positioning 115, 118; propelling 124–125; punching the ball 112, 114, 118; punting 122; stance 114; throwing 114; tipping 41, 119; training 36–37, 113–114

halfbacks 77–78, 87, 91; center 15, 73–74, 77, 80, 82, 91; wingers 74–75; *see also* midfielders
head passes 7, 29
heading 49–50
hypothermia 23

injuries: ankle sprains 22, 29; knee problems 22, 29; torn muscles 22

jogging 28

kick-ball 12, 82
kick-off 82, 91, 107
kicks 7, 29; back-heel 41, 163; blind-cross 39; chip 165; corner 91, 94–95, 108, 117; duck-bill instep 38, 156; free 108, 182, 189, 190;

front-volley 38; goal 93, 108; half-volley 38; instep 38, 39, 62–63, 101, 128, 138, 143, 145, 155, 156–158; instep-stride 41, 163; once-on 3, 65, 139; outside-of-the-foot 39, 154; penalty 101, 188, 190; push pass (aka inside-of-the-foot) 29, 38, 39, 62, 63, 64–65, 132, 139, 143, 145, 146; scissors 160; shooting (or shot on goal) 96, 132, 142; toe-poke 41; under-the-body instep 39; volley 39, 128, 139, 158–160, 168

laws 7, 179: the ball (II.) 181; ball in and out of play (IX.) 186; corner-kick (XVII.) 192; duration of the game (VII.) 184; the field of play (I.) 179; fouls and misconduct (XII.) 187; free-kick (XIII.) 189; goal-kick (XVI.) 192; linesmen (VI.) 184; offside (XI.) 186; penalty kick (XIV.) 190; number of players (III.) 181; players' equipment (IV.) 282; referees (V.) 183; method of scoring (X.) 186; the start of play (VIII.) 185; throw-in (XV.) 191
leadership 2, 3; fostering of 9–15; league 10; negative 10–11; self-awareness 9; self-control 9
league 8, 10, 13–17, 103; charter 34–35; control of 32–34; officers 153
lines-persons 104, 106; *see also* referees
long-ball 2, 5, 12

managing 8; *see also* coaches
midfielders 76; *see also* halfbacks

negative aspects of the game 11, 13, 153
negative practices 33

officials *see* referees
offside 69, 83, 106, 108; laws 186

once-on *see* kicks
one-half game rule 6
orange designator 23

parents' participation 17–20, 34–35
pass 84–85; head 7; self-pass 139; *see also* kicks
physician 86
players 71, 91; characteristics 71; control of 15–16; liabilities 71–76; positions 71; professionals 42–44, 50; style, with 41–43; substitute 6, 16–17, 182; time in the game 17; *see also* laws
plays 91
poor quality play 12–13
positions *see* specific positions
practice guidelines 27–30; *see also* drills, homework; drills, practice
practice *see* drills
preparation for games 107
psychology, child 18

rebound board 12, 49, 127, 167; fabrication 131
referees (officials) 15, 53, 55, 103, 110, 183; coach's evaluation of 108–109; control of 13, 14, 103; coordinator 10, 13, 103, 107, 109; evaluation of coaches 105; laws 183; preparation for games, 104, 107; program 13; three- and two-person systems 105, 107; trainer 10, 13
remedial program 153
rule, advantage 53; *see also* laws
running 21, 29, 52

scoring 100, 137
scrimmage games 29
self-awareness 9
self-confidence 5
self-control 2–3, 5, 9, 14–15, 31, 90
shielding 4, 7, 14, 29, 47, 48, 50–58, 90, 132, 146; dribbling, and 47; drill 52; immediately upon receipt of the ball 51; on the touch line 56; turning 48, 54; trapping, and 134
short-ball 2, 5, 8
shoulder charging *see* tackling
skill levels, by age 25–42
skills 6–7, 29; basic 29, 38, 45, 132, 153; *see also* specific skill
stopper back 79
stretching 21, 29
substitution coordinator 17
substitute *see* players
sweeperback 72, 79

tackling 7, 31, 59, 172; shoulder-charge 6, 10, 10–21, 38–39, 90, 132, 176; sliding 38, 88, 173–174; sliding-block 38, 174–176; standing-block 41, 172; two-person 59, 176–177
televised games 35
throw-ins 7, 29, 66–69, 91, 93, 108; laws 191; *see also* drills
training: jogging 28; running backwards 29; stretching 21, 29; warm-up exercises 21, 29; wind-sprints 29; *see also* practice guidelines
trapping 7, 29, 38, 48–49, 90, 128, 132, 133–135; basic 48; body 61–62, 133, 135; calf 41, 169; chest 65, 133, 135; drills, practice 132, 133; drills, homework 137; dropping-ball 39; head 39, 167; in front of the goal 97, 142; inside-of-the-foot 36, 165–167, 170; outside-of-foot 170; pseudo 171; shielding, and 134; side-of-the-thigh 41, 168; top-of-the-thigh 41, 169; under-the-foot 138, 167
turning 48, 54

United States Soccer Federation 179

verbal assist 6
violence 10, 103
volley *see* kicks

wall pass 91–93, 145
walls, setting up 99
water 22
wind sprints 29

wingers 73–76, 83, 94, 96; defensive
    73, 79, 83, 94, 95; forward or
    attacking 75–76, 82; *see also* for-
    wards; half backs